The Be~~~~
Better Golf
Number 3

Jack Nicklaus

CORONET BOOKS
Hodder and Stoughton

Copyright © 1967, 1968 by Ohio Publications Inc.
Copyright © 1969 by Jack Nicklaus
Coronet edition 1971
Twelfth impression 1982

_____

This book is sold subject to the condition that
it shall not, by way of trade or otherwise, be
lent, re-sold, hired out or otherwise circulated
without the publisher's prior consent in any
form of binding or cover other than that in
which this is published and without a similar
condition including this condition being
imposed on the subsequent purchaser.

Printed and bound in Great Britain for
Hodder and Stoughton Paperbacks, a
division of Hodder and Stoughton Ltd,
Mill Road, Dunton Green, Sevenoaks,
Kent (Editorial Office : 47 Bedford
Square, London, WC1 3DP) by
Richard Clay (The Chaucer Press) Ltd,
Bungay, Suffolk

ISBN 0 340 15475 6

CONTENTS

INTRODUCTION

One of the reasons I enjoy participating in this illustrated golf instruction series is that it gives me the rare opportunity to address myself to a vast number of golfers all at once. As a professional, I am in the business of playing golf tournaments. This is virtually a year-round job and it doesn't leave me much time for personalized, individual instruction.

Another reason I favor this particular method is that I believe by studying the line drawings that appear in this book you can learn to mirror correct form and technique. So much of golf is learned by observing others, and this has proved to be a beneficial way of improving the way we play. We can see movies or still photographs of ourselves, which help us to correct the flaws in our game.

Recently I read a story about Jim Thorpe, one of the all-time great athletes this nation has produced. As a high school kid, Thorpe was once spotted by his high school coach jumping over the high bar, which was set at a pretty good height. The coach came over and said he didn't know Thorpe had been practicing the high jump. Thorpe said it was the first time he had ever tried it. "But if I see someone else do it, then I can do it," he explained.

Well, we all aren't Jim Thorpe with his amazing reflexes and athletic ability, but all of us do have the ability to learn by watching. This is why I recommend these illustrated panels as a way of learning. Certainly they should be used as a supplement to the instruction you get from a qualified professional, but I think they can stand on their own merit.

I've organized this book in a way I think will benefit golfers of all handicaps. There are probably some low-handicappers who may choose to skip over certain parts here that seem elementary to them. Skip if you want to, but first have a quick look just to make sure you're not overlooking some small problem you're still having with your game. High-handicappers should overlook nothing. Just keep reading and learning—and, above all, keep swinging. That's the only way to chop down those extra strokes. And that, in the final analysis, is what the game is all about.

JACK NICKLAUS

CHAPTER 1
The Masters and Me

I've heard it said that the Augusta National, site of the annual Masters golf championship, was built for a big hitter like Jack Nicklaus. If this implies that the comparatively long, wide fairways and large-size greens afford a long hitter the opportunity to let out the shaft, then this is probably correct.

The Augusta National does favor big hitters such as I. But this in no way means it's an easy course to conquer; on the contrary, it is probably one of the most perfectly designed courses offering a fair test of golf anywhere in the world. Those deep and inviting fairways are loaded with severe penalties for any golfer bold enough to throw caution to the winds.

In the six years that I have been privileged to play in this tournament, dreamed up by the great Bob Jones, the Augusta National has been very kind to me. I have won The Masters three times (in 1963, 1965, and 1966), hold the tournament record of 274, and am the only player ever to win it in consecutive years. Only my good buddy, Arnie Palmer, has won The Masters as many as four times, and my first aim in 1969 was to match that feat.

Truly, The Masters is one of the most prestigious golf championships in the world, ranking with the U.S. Open, the British Open, and the PGA Championship as the Big Four in professional golf. It's such an honor just to be invited to play in The Masters, much less to win it, that there is a saying that pros would rather win The Open but play in The Masters.

This spring I will be trying for my fourth Masters. I know the course as well as I know my way around my own living room. I carry notes with me around the course, but there are still hidden dangers that can upset anyone's blueprint for victory. But if I am going to win it again, the key will lie in the six holes I have included in this first section. I hope I can play up to my game plan.

THE '68 MASTERS
MY PLAN FOR NO. 1 · 400 YDS. PAR 4

THERE IS NOTHING LIKE A GOOD START IN **ANY** TOURNAMENT.... SO I'll TRY TO PLAY THIS HOLE THE WAY THAT I HAVE THE MOST CONFIDENCE IN. I LIKE TO DRIVE SLIGHTLY TO THE **LEFT**, EVEN THOUGH THE BEST APPROACH IS FROM THE **RIGHT**... BECAUSE THE PIN IS USUALLY TUCKED AWAY ON THE LEFT. HOWEVER, THERE IS A LIKELIHOOD THAT A SHOT TO THE LEFT SIDE OF THIS GREEN (ESPECIALLY A DRAW) WILL BOUNCE RIGHT OFF AND WIND UP IN A BOGEY POSITION.

I FAVOR A MORE OR LESS **STRAIGHT-ON** SHOT AT THE PIN (MAY-BE SLIGHTLY TO THE RIGHT) FROM A LEFT FAIRWAY POSITION.... GIVING ME ALMOST THE WHOLE GREEN ON THE RIGHT.

MY PLAN FOR NO. 7 · 365 YDS. PAR 4

THIS IS ONE OF THE MOST "ACCURACY DEMANDING" HOLES ON THE COURSE... AND ONE OF THE BEST HOLES IN GOLF. IT'S NOT A LONG HOLE, BUT REQUIRES TWO GOOD SHOTS TO PUT YOU NEAR THE PIN IN BIRDIE POSITION.

IF THE FAIRWAY IS WET, I'll PLAY A DRIVER FROM THE TEE.... AS THE BALL WILL STOP QUICKLY AND NOT "RUN" INTO ANY TROUBLE. UNDER HARD CONDITIONS, I'll FAVOR THE MORE ACCURATE 3-WOOD. FOR EITHER STRATEGY, I'll TRY TO HIT A CONTROLLED LEFT-TO-RIGHT FADE.

THE 9-IRON OR WEDGE APPROACH MUST BE HIT VERY HIGH (AND WITH PLENTY OF SPIN) TO A DIFFICULT GREEN TO "HOLD." THE IDEAL SHOT WILL BE JUST OVER THE FRONT BUNKER.

MY PLAN FOR NO. 11 · 445 YDS. PAR 4

THE TEE SHOT POSITION IS RATHER OPTIONAL HERE... DEPENDING ON HOW YOU WANT TO HIT YOUR SECOND SHOT. THE LEFT SIDE OF THE FAIRWAY PROVIDES A LEVEL LIE, BUT THE SECOND SHOT IS PRACTICALLY OVER WATER. TOO MANY TOURNAMENTS HAVE BEEN LOST ON THIS VERY HOLE WITH A DISASTROUS SECOND SHOT.

THE RIGHT FAIRWAY IS SAFER... WITH THE "PERCENTAGE" APPROACH FALLING SHORT AND ROLLING — GOING IN FROM RIGHT TO LEFT. IT'S ONE OF THE FEW HOLES IN GOLF THAT YOU DON'T WANT TO HIT, BECAUSE SUCH A LONG SHOT COULD EASILY KICK OR ROLL RIGHT INTO THE WATER. I CALL THIS A 4½ HOLE... AND DEPEND UPON A GOOD CHIP OR A LONG PUTT TO GET ME CLOSE ENOUGH TO PAR.

THIS IS ONE OF THE TOUGHEST PAR 3'S IN GOLF. THE GREEN IS GUARDED BY RAE'S CREEK IN THE FRONT; AND BY SLOPING TRAPS IN THE REAR. WIND CONDITIONS ARE VERY IMPORTANT AND MOST OFTEN DICTATE THE TYPE OF SHOT THAT I WILL HIT (USUALLY WITH A 6- OR 7-IRON). I NORMALLY TRY TO FADE THE BALL IN... AIMING AT THE LEFT PART OF THE GREEN.

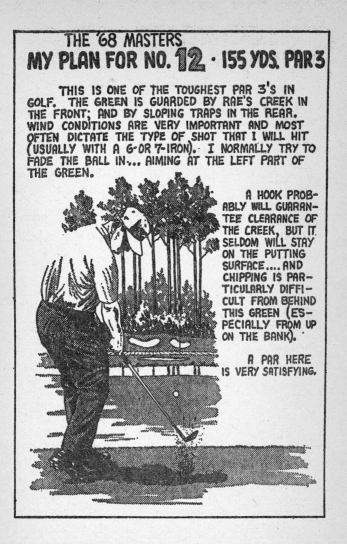

A HOOK PROBABLY WILL GUARANTEE CLEARANCE OF THE CREEK, BUT IT SELDOM WILL STAY ON THE PUTTING SURFACE.... AND CHIPPING IS PARTICULARLY DIFFICULT FROM BEHIND THIS GREEN (ESPECIALLY FROM UP ON THE BANK).

A PAR HERE IS VERY SATISFYING.

THE '68 MASTERS
MY PLAN FOR NO. 15:
520 YDS. PAR 5

MY KEY THOUGHT FOR THIS HOLE WILL BE TO LEAVE THE SHORTEST POSSIBLE SECOND SHOT... SO I'll TRY TO HIT MY TEE SHOT AS HARD AS I CAN. I'll PLAY A RIGHT-TO-LEFT SHOT TO GET AS MUCH ROLL AS POSSIBLE... AND, NATURALLY, TRY TO AVOID THE TREES IN THE FAIRWAY.

A BIG DRIVE WILL MEAN THAT I CAN HIT AN IRON TO THE GREEN – WHICH IS GUARDED BY WATER BOTH IN FRONT AND TO THE LEFT REAR.

I'll ATTEMPT A HIGH APPROACH THAT WILL HOLD ... AND IF I DO MISS THE GREEN, I WANT TO DO SO ON THE RIGHT. THIS COULD RESULT IN A DOWN-HILL CHIP, BUT I WOULD HAVE A MUCH BETTER CHANCE AT A BIRDIE 4 FROM THERE THAN ON THE LEFT... WHERE A BOGEY 6 (OR WORSE) WOULD COME EASY!

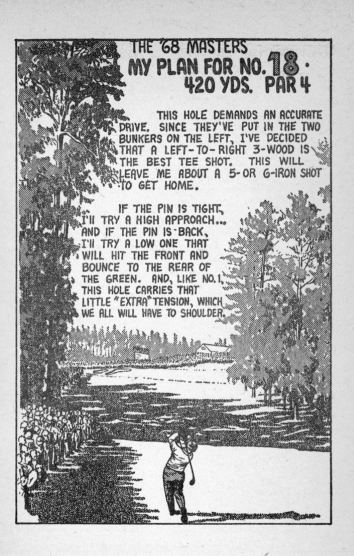

THE '68 MASTERS
MY PLAN FOR NO. 18 :
420 YDS. PAR 4

THIS HOLE DEMANDS AN ACCURATE DRIVE. SINCE THEY'VE PUT IN THE TWO BUNKERS ON THE LEFT, I'VE DECIDED THAT A LEFT-TO-RIGHT 3-WOOD IS THE BEST TEE SHOT. THIS WILL LEAVE ME ABOUT A 5- OR 6-IRON SHOT TO GET HOME.

IF THE PIN IS TIGHT, I'll TRY A HIGH APPROACH... AND IF THE PIN IS BACK, I'll TRY A LOW ONE THAT WILL HIT THE FRONT AND BOUNCE TO THE REAR OF THE GREEN. AND, LIKE NO. 1, THIS HOLE CARRIES THAT LITTLE "EXTRA" TENSION, WHICH WE ALL WILL HAVE TO SHOULDER.

15

CHAPTER 2

Developing the Proper Mental Attitude

Stubbornness and pride are two of the biggest obstacles to playing your best golf. I have seen too many hardheaded golfers throw away shots—and consequently tournaments—because of these all-too-human qualities.

You should remember that a golf course is laid out to reward you for playing proper shots well and to penalize you for making imprudent shots. This is why I've always maintained that your toughest opponent in golf is not necessarily the man you're playing against, but yourself. Not having a good mental attitude can make you your own worst enemy.

Developing such an attitude falls into several specific areas. One of them is the ability to assess intelligently the golfing problem confronting you before you make your shot. Study the layout in front of you. Weigh the consequences of a poor shot or, worse, of using bad judgment. Look for the safe way when possible.

Another common failing I find among a large number of golfers is their attempts to make the impossible shot. At given moments they suddenly feel they can make a certain shot they never before have pulled off; they overreach themselves. You should always play within your own known capabilities. Be realistic.

And a final flaw prevalent in golfers of all handicaps is a tendency to get down on themselves when things are not going their way. They lose confidence, possibly because they've just made a bad shot on the previous hole or because their opponent has got them "psyched." When this happens, you really are beaten. That's the time you should blot out mistakes you can't undo and bear down. Play the course, not your playing opponent.

There have been countless times in my own tournament experience when pure determination—and good golf—brought me back from certain defeat. But the instance that always inspires me was the time Bobby Cruickshank came back from being 11 down with 13 holes to play to Al Watrous in the 1932 PGA Championship and won the match. That's perseverance.

DEVELOP CONFIDENCE

FAITH IN ONE'S OWN ABILITY IS PERHAPS THE GREATEST SINGLE GIFT A GOLFER CAN HAVE. I HAVE NEVER SEEN A TRUE CHAMPION IN ANY SPORT WHO DID NOT HAVE AN IMPREGNABLE ARMOR OF "BELIEF IN HIMSELF."

IN GOLF THIS IS THE RESULT OF CONSCIENTIOUS, CONSTRUCTIVE PRACTICE UNTIL A REPERTOIRE OF ALMOST "AUTOMATIC" SHOTS IS ATTAINED.

JUST REMEMBER THAT EVERY GOLF PROFESSIONAL YOU SEE OUT ON THE P.G.A. TOUR IS THE PRODUCT OF THOUSANDS OF HOURS OF PRACTICE.

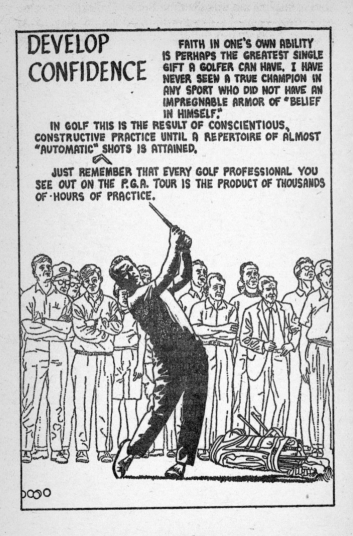

DEVELOP A MENTAL YARDSTICK

I HAVE ENCOURAGED "PART-STRENGTH" SHOTS (ONE-FOURTH, ONE-HALF, THREE-QUARTER SHOTS) TO DEVELOP A SENSE OF FEEL. IT ALSO TEACHES A SPECIFIC LENGTH SWING TO ACCOMMODATE A SPECIFIC LENGTH (IN YARDAGE) SHOT, WHICH CARRIES OVER TO FULL SHOTS.

BY VISUALIZING AND PLANNING THE SHOT WHILE PLAYING, YOU CAN REACH A POSITIVE DECISION OF WHAT CLUB TO USE AND HOW TO USE IT. YOUR MIND WILL BE FREE TO CONCENTRATE ON THE EXECUTION OF THE SHOT AND DIRECTION OF THE SHOT.

BEING OBSERVANT PAYS OFF

THE CARDINAL RULE OF "PLAYING FOR POSITION" IS VIRTUALLY IMPOSSIBLE IF YOU DO NOT KNOW THE APPROXIMATE PIN POSITION ON EACH HOLE. OFTEN TIMES DETERMINATION OF PIN POSITION IS DIFFICULT FROM THE HITTING AREA, SO TRY TO MAKE A MENTAL NOTE OF THE EXACT POSITION OF THE PINS ON UPCOMING HOLES WHEN YOU PASS ADJACENT TO THEM OR WHENEVER THEY COME INTO VIEW.

AN OBSERVING MOMENT OR TWO ON ONE HOLE CAN REALLY PAY OFF ON "ANOTHER" HOLE!

SIZING UP YOUR OPPONENT

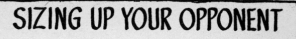

A WISE OLD PROVERB SAYS: "A SECRET DISBELIEF IN THE ENEMY'S PLAY IS VERY USEFUL." THIS IS PARTICULARLY TRUE IN MATCH PLAY...WHERE AWE AND FEAR OF ANOTHER'S "GAME" CAN BEAT YOU BEFORE YOU TEE IT UP ON NO. 1. IF YOU CANNOT MENTALLY EXCEL...AT LEAST BELIEVE YOU'RE HIS EQUAL, REMEMBERING THAT BEFORE THE ROUND IS OVER ...HE WILL CERTAINLY SUFFER SOME MIS-HIT SHOTS AND/OR BAD LUCK LIKE EVERY GOLFER DOES!

PLAY PERCENTAGE GOLF

EVERY GOLFER SHOULD HAVE AT LEAST A GENERAL PLAN FOR ATTACKING A HOLE. YOU SHOULD, INDEED, SELECT WHAT, IN YOUR JUDGMENT, IS THE BEST AND SAFEST ROUTE FROM TEE TO GREEN. COMPLETE KNOWLEDGE OF YOUR FACULTIES AND LIMITATIONS IS A "MUST" IN THIS RESPECT.

SO AS SPECIAL SITUATIONS ARISE ALONG THE WAY, BE ABLE TO ANALYZE THEM ... CALCULATE THE ODDS ... AND MAKE YOUR PLAY WITH INTELLIGENCE AND CONFIDENCE.

MOVING THE BALL FROM TROUBLE

I NEVER TRY TO HIT THE BALL STRAIGHT, BUT ALWAYS AIM TO ONE SIDE OF THE FAIRWAY AND TRY TO MOVE THE BALL TOWARD THE MIDDLE. MOVING THE BALL AWAY FROM TROUBLE LESSENS THE CHANCE OF FINISHING IN A BAD POSITION FOR THE NEXT SHOT.

I PREFER TO MOVE THE BALL FROM LEFT TO RIGHT BECAUSE I FEEL THAT A FADE GENERALLY KEEPS THE BALL IN PLAY UNDER MOST CONDITIONS. HOWEVER, WHEN THE SHOT DEMANDS IT, I WILL TRY FOR A RIGHT-TO-LEFT DRAW.

DEVELOP A PROPER ATTITUDE
·ON TOURNAMENT PLAY·

A PROPER MENTAL ATTITUDE WILL CARRY A GOLFER A LONG WAY IN CLUB TOURNAMENTS...THOSE EVENTS WHICH TEND TO UPSET THE GOOD MANAGEMENT AND LUCID THINKING PORTRAYED DURING NORMAL PLAY.

WALTER HAGEN ONCE SAID THAT HE ALWAYS ASSUMED AT THE BEGINNING OF ANY ROUND THAT HE WOULD PROBABLY MAKE THREE OR FOUR MISTAKES, AND HE WAS THUS MENTALLY PREPARED TO·TAKE THEM IN STRIDE. SO DON'T TENSE UP IN FEAR OF ERROR. JUST HIT AWAY WITH THE DETERMINATION TO SHRUG OFF ANY MISTAKES, AND TO MAKE UP FOR ANY BY IN-TELLIGENT APPLICATION OF GOLFING PRINCIPLES.

THINK POSITIVE AFTER A BAD SHOT

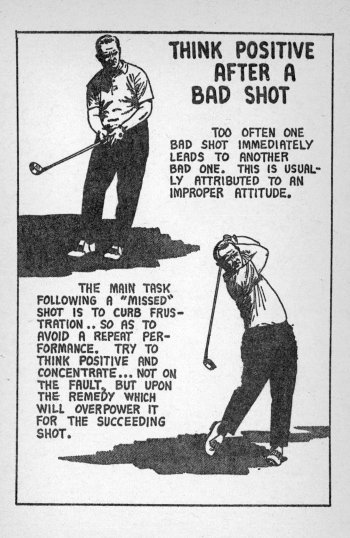

TOO OFTEN ONE BAD SHOT IMMEDIATELY LEADS TO ANOTHER BAD ONE. THIS IS USUALLY ATTRIBUTED TO AN IMPROPER ATTITUDE.

THE MAIN TASK FOLLOWING A "MISSED" SHOT IS TO CURB FRUSTRATION .. SO AS TO AVOID A REPEAT PERFORMANCE. TRY TO THINK POSITIVE AND CONCENTRATE... NOT ON THE FAULT, BUT UPON THE REMEDY WHICH WILL OVERPOWER IT FOR THE SUCCEEDING SHOT.

DEFEATING THE O.B. HANDICAP

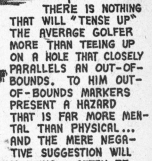

THERE IS NOTHING THAT WILL "TENSE UP" THE AVERAGE GOLFER MORE THAN TEEING UP ON A HOLE THAT CLOSELY PARALLELS AN OUT-OF-BOUNDS. TO HIM OUT-OF-BOUNDS MARKERS PRESENT A HAZARD THAT IS FAR MORE MENTAL THAN PHYSICAL... AND THE MERE NEGATIVE SUGGESTION WILL CAUSE HIM TO ALTER HIS SWING... OFTEN RESULTING IN **HITTING** THE BALL RIGHT OUT OF THE COURSE.

TEE UP NEAREST THE BOUNDARY AND HIT <u>AWAY</u> FROM IT.. USING YOUR NORMAL SWING.

JUDGING DISTANCE

JUDGING DISTANCE IS PARTICULARLY DIFFICULT WHEN PLAYING A STRANGE COURSE. LOOK FOR THINGS THAT OFFER SIZE AND PERSPECTIVE COMPARISON -- TRAPS, SURROUNDING TREES, HEIGHT OF THE PIN, PLAYERS ON THE GREEN, ETC.

MANY GOLFERS USE THE "PROGRESSION" METHOD: SIGHT AN OBJECT THAT IS WEDGE DISTANCE (THIS IS USUALLY QUITE EASY), THEN PICK OUT OTHER OBJECTS THAT ARE PROGRESSIVELY CLOSER TO THE GREEN. BY DROPPING DOWN ONE LOFTED CLUB FOR EACH 10-YARD SEGMENT YOUR SIGHTINGS PROGRESS FROM THE BALL, YOU ARRIVE AT THE CORRECT CLUB WITH WHICH TO REACH THE GREEN.

FOR THE BEGINNER:
STRIVE FOR CONFIDENCE WHEN PUTTING

MOST PUTTING TROUBLES STEM FROM THE LACK OF CONFIDENCE... FROM BEING JUST PLAIN **SCARED.**

A PUTT IS LIKE ANY OTHER SHOT IN THAT IT MUST BE PLANNED WITH A POSITIVE PROCEDURE. TAKE YOUR TIME.... STUDY THE LINE, BREAK AND SPEED REQUIRED, AND STICK WITH YOUR PLAN. BE <u>CONFIDENT</u> OF SUCCESS AND IMAGINE HOW THE BALL WILL LOOK AS IT DROPS INTO THE CUP.

A TIME TO PLAY IT COZY

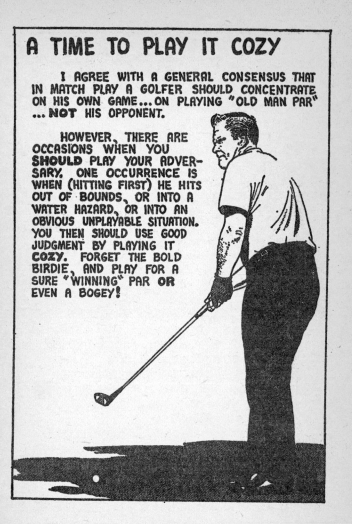

I AGREE WITH A GENERAL CONSENSUS THAT IN MATCH PLAY A GOLFER SHOULD CONCENTRATE ON HIS OWN GAME...ON PLAYING "OLD MAN PAR" ...**NOT** HIS OPPONENT.

HOWEVER, THERE ARE OCCASIONS WHEN YOU **SHOULD** PLAY YOUR ADVERSARY. ONE OCCURRENCE IS WHEN (HITTING FIRST) HE HITS OUT OF BOUNDS, OR INTO A WATER HAZARD, OR INTO AN OBVIOUS UNPLAYABLE SITUATION. YOU THEN SHOULD USE GOOD JUDGMENT BY PLAYING IT **COZY**. FORGET THE BOLD BIRDIE, AND PLAY FOR A SURE "WINNING" PAR **OR** EVEN A BOGEY!

CHAPTER 3

A Refresher Course

No matter what your handicap, you can always use a refresher course in the fundamentals, particularly in the early spring after you've had a long layoff. Even touring pros find their games accumulate a certain amount of winter rust and they return to the practice tee to put things back in order.

The big difference, though, is that we generally know what to look for. We know our games inside out and where we've gone stale. But the average recreational golfer can have problems in almost any phase of his game. One season it can be with his driver, another with his short game. So if you've had a sizable rest between seasons, the best thing you can do is look your game over from top to bottom and see what changes have occurred during the respite.

Oddly enough, many recreational golfers claim they hit their woods better than they thought they could the first time they return to the course. This is probably because they're relaxed—the tensions they built up in their games the year before are no longer there and they can hit more freely. This can be quite deceiving. It doesn't necessarily mean that through some magic rest formula they have corrected some basic flaw that was present in their grip or swing.

If you hit from the top last season and did nothing about it, the chances are strong you will be doing the same thing again this year. Errors have a way of coming back to haunt you when they go unchecked.

The only thing you can do about eliminating these problems is to work on them. Often this means going back to your professional—it's certainly the quickest way. But in this chapter I've returned to the basics, which is where most of our golf problems originate. To some of you it might seem like returning to kindergarten, but even the best of us have to do that once in a while.

FOR THE BEGINNER:
WHAT TYPE OF GRIP?

PERSONAL PREFERENCE WILL DETERMINE WHAT GRIP TO USE. I PREFER THE **INTERLOCKING**... AND I BELIEVE THAT IT IS THE EASIEST TO LEARN. IT <u>LINKS</u> THE HANDS TOGETHER AUTOMATICALLY.

THE **OVERLAPPING** (AND MOST POPULAR) KNITS THE HANDS TOGETHER IN AN ARTIFICIAL SORT OF WAY... BY HOOKING THE SMALL RIGHT FINGER OVER THE KNUCKLE OF THE LEFT FOREFINGER.

AND THEN THERE'S THE **FULL FINGER GRIP**, WHICH OBVIOUSLY DOESN'T SEEM TO MOLD THE HANDS TOGETHER IN PROPER UNISON.

HOWEVER, ALL THREE GRIPS ARE SOUND. THEY DIFFER ONLY IN LINKAGE.

THE GRIP PRESSURE POINTS

MY GRIP IS **FIRM** IN ALL FINGERS, BUT I FEEL PRESSURE EMPHASIZED IN THE LAST TWO FINGERS AND THE PAD OF THE LEFT HAND... AND IN THE THUMB AND INDEX FINGER OF THE RIGHT. THE AMOUNT OF THIS PRESSURE WILL VARY WITH THE INDIVIDUAL GOLFER (JUST DON'T INHIBIT FREE-HINGEING WRISTS BY GRIPPING **TOO** TIGHT.)

I AM NOT CONSCIOUS OF ANY CHANGE IN GRIP PRESSURE DURING THE SWING. I FIRM UP MY GRIP SLIGHTLY JUST BEFORE STARTING THE SWING, AND I KEEP IT FIRM THROUGHOUT.

FOR THE BEGINNER:
DEVELOP A ONE-PIECE BACKSWING

TRY TO MOVE THE ENTIRE LEFT SIDE AWAY FROM THE BALL AT ONCE, WITH NO ONE PART OF THE BODY DOMINATING THE TURN.

A GOOD WAY TO ACHIEVE THIS "ONE-PIECE START" IS TO CONCENTRATE ON TAKING THE CLUB BACK VERY SLOWLY DURING THE FIRST 6 OR 8 INCHES FROM THE BALL. BE PARTICULARLY SURE THAT THERE IS NO EARLY WRIST ACTION... SO AS TO KEEP THE STRAIGHT LINE FORMED BY THE LEFT ARM AND SHAFT UNBROKEN.

PROPER WEIGHT DISTRIBUTION AT ADDRESS

I FEEL THAT MY WEIGHT AT ADDRESS IS EVENLY DIVIDED BETWEEN BOTH FEET AND ALSO BETWEEN THE HEEL AND BALL OF EACH FOOT.

THERE IS A PRESSURE POINT ON THE INSIDE OF MY RIGHT FOOT (BOTH HEEL AND BALL). I ACTUALLY BRACE MYSELF WITH THIS FOOT BY PUSHING SLIGHTLY TOWARD THE LEFT SIDE, BUT AT THE SAME TIME MAKING CERTAIN THAT MY BODY IS LARGELY BEHIND THE BALL.

STRAIGHT LEFT ARM AT ADDRESS

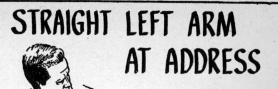

WHEN YOU TAKE YOUR STANCE AT ADDRESS PLACE YOUR HANDS IN SUCH A WAY THAT THE CLUBSHAFT AND LEFT ARM FORM A STRAIGHT LINE, WITH YOUR HANDS SLIGHTLY AHEAD OF THE BALL. THIS STRAIGHT ARM ALIGNMENT WILL NOT ONLY FACILITATE THE "ONE PIECE" TAKEAWAY, BUT WILL INCREASE YOUR SWING ARC.

ALSO, STARTING WITH THE HANDS AHEAD OF THE BALL WILL AID IN ACHIEVING THE DESIRED RELATIVE POSITION AT IMPACT.

THE ROLE OF THE WAGGLE

IT IS DIFFICULT TO PICK OUT ONE PARTICULAR INSTANT WHEN THE BACKSWING STARTS. I FEEL THAT THE "WAGGLE" AND THE FIRST MOVEMENT IN THE ACTUAL SWING ARE ALL A PART OF A CONTINUOUS MOTION.

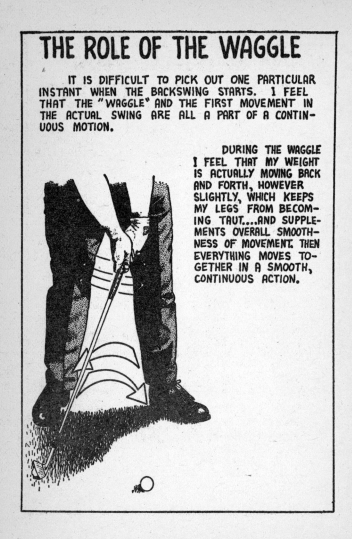

DURING THE WAGGLE I FEEL THAT MY WEIGHT IS ACTUALLY MOVING BACK AND FORTH, HOWEVER SLIGHTLY, WHICH KEEPS MY LEGS FROM BECOMING TAUT....AND SUPPLEMENTS OVERALL SMOOTHNESS OF MOVEMENT. THEN EVERYTHING MOVES TOGETHER IN A SMOOTH, CONTINUOUS ACTION.

SETTING UP THE BACKSWING

IN ORDER TO PROMOTE A FREER, EASIER BODY TURN... I ADVOCATE A SLIGHT INCLINING, OR SETTING-IN OF THE RIGHT KNEE AT ADDRESS.

WEIGHT THEN SHIFTS EASILY, AND REMAINS ON THE <u>INSIDE</u> OF THE RIGHT FOOT (WHICH HELPS TO LOCK THE RIGHT KNEE AND PREVENT LATERAL HIP MOTION, OR SWAY).

YOU NEED SIMPLY TO **TURN** YOUR BODY TO BE CORRECTLY IN POSITION BEHIND THE BALL.

THE GRADUAL WRISTCOCK

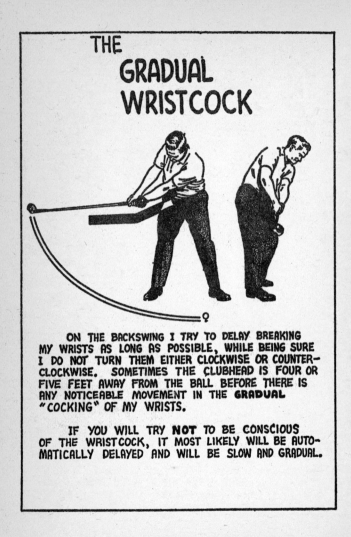

ON THE BACKSWING I TRY TO DELAY BREAKING MY WRISTS AS LONG AS POSSIBLE, WHILE BEING SURE I DO NOT TURN THEM EITHER CLOCKWISE OR COUNTER-CLOCKWISE. SOMETIMES THE CLUBHEAD IS FOUR OR FIVE FEET AWAY FROM THE BALL BEFORE THERE IS ANY NOTICEABLE MOVEMENT IN THE **GRADUAL** "COCKING" OF MY WRISTS.

IF YOU WILL TRY **NOT** TO BE CONSCIOUS OF THE WRISTCOCK, IT MOST LIKELY WILL BE AUTO-MATICALLY DELAYED AND WILL BE SLOW AND GRADUAL.

FOR THE BEGINNER:
ROLE OF
THE HANDS
ON THE
BACKSWING

IN MAKING A
PROPER BACKSWING,
TRY TO REMEMBER
THAT YOUR **HANDS**
<u>DO</u> <u>NOT</u> INITIATE
THE TAKEAWAY, BUT
SERVE ONLY TO HOLD
THE CLUB.. PROVIDING THE LINK-
AGE FOR THE ONE-PIECE UNIT
OF THE CLUBSHAFT AND LEFT
ARM.

WITH THIS POINT IN MIND, THE BACKSWING
SIMPLY BECOMES A MATTER OF THE BODY TURNING
AROUND THE HEAD. THE HANDS WILL BREAK AUTO-
MATICALLY WHEN THE PROPER TIME ARRIVES.

FOR THE BEGINNER:
SHOULDER AND HIP TURN

REGARDLESS OF CLUB OR TYPE OF SHOT, ALWAYS REMEMBER THAT YOUR **SHOULDERS** MUST TURN FARTHER THAN YOUR HIPS. IN MAKING A FULL BODY TURN, YOUR SHOULDERS SHOULD TURN <u>AS FAR AS THEY WILL GO</u> (AND STILL MAINTAIN A STEADY HEAD)... PREFERABLY UNTIL YOUR BACK FACES THE TARGET; BUT YOUR HIPS, SOMEWHAT RESTRAINED, SHOULD MAKE ABOUT HALF THAT TURN. THIS CREATES A STORED UP "TENSION" BETWEEN THE HIPS AND SHOULDERS WHICH WILL HELP YOU TO START YOUR DOWNSWING... AN AUTOMATIC "HELP" IN PULLING YOU DOWN IN TO THE BALL.

KEEP A FIRM GRIP THROUGHOUT

A REQUISITE FOR CONSISTENT GOLF IS TO MAINTAIN A CONSTANT PRESSURE ON THE GRIP **THROUGHOUT** THE SWING, EVEN <u>AFTER</u> THE BALL IS STRUCK!

ALLOWING THE HANDS TO LOOSEN JUST AFTER IMPACT MAY NOT RESULT IN LOSS OF CLUBHEAD SPEED, BUT IT WILL CAUSE A LOSS OF FIRMNESS AND CONTROL TO THE SHOT.... AND THE LOOSENESS MIGHT CREEP **BACK** INTO THE EARLIER PHASES OF YOUR SWING.

THE THUMB AND PALM CHECK

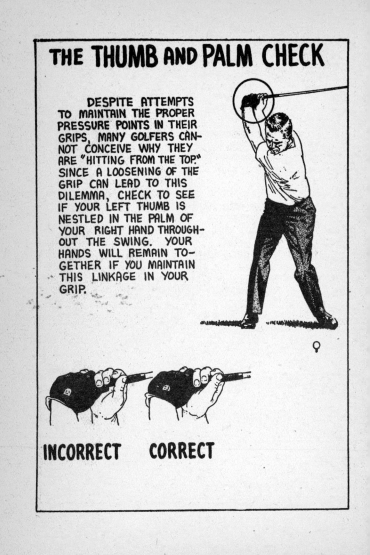

DESPITE ATTEMPTS TO MAINTAIN THE PROPER PRESSURE POINTS IN THEIR GRIPS, MANY GOLFERS CANNOT CONCEIVE WHY THEY ARE "HITTING FROM THE TOP" SINCE A LOOSENING OF THE GRIP CAN LEAD TO THIS DILEMMA, CHECK TO SEE IF YOUR LEFT THUMB IS NESTLED IN THE PALM OF YOUR RIGHT HAND THROUGHOUT THE SWING. YOUR HANDS WILL REMAIN TOGETHER IF YOU MAINTAIN THIS LINKAGE IN YOUR GRIP.

INCORRECT   CORRECT

FOR THE BEGINNER:
KEEP YOUR HEAD STILL!

NEARLY ALL BEGINNERS ARE CONSTANTLY REMINDED TO KEEP THEIR EYE ON THE BALL. THIS IS CERTAINLY GOOD ADVICE, BUT IT IS MERELY ANOTHER WAY OF SAYING "KEEP YOUR HEAD STILL". CERTAINLY BY KEEPING YOUR EYE ON THE BALL YOU SHOULD FIND IT EASIER TO RESIST A PREMATURE LIFTING OR TURNING OF YOUR HEAD.

MOVING YOUR HEAD DURING THE SWING IS A QUICK WAY TO DISRUPT YOUR SWING ARC... AND CAN BECOME A HABIT THAT IS DIFFICULT TO BREAK!

FOR THE BEGINNER:
THE "WHY" OF SHOTS

BEFORE A PERSON CAN REALLY GET IN-TO THE "HEART" OF LEARNING GOLF, HE SHOULD STUDY THE CAUSE AND EFFECT OF SHOTS HE WILL BE HITTING. BEFORE YOU CAN CORRECT A HOOK, SLICE, PUSH OR PULL, YOU SHOULD FIRST UNDERSTAND **WHY** THEY OCCUR.

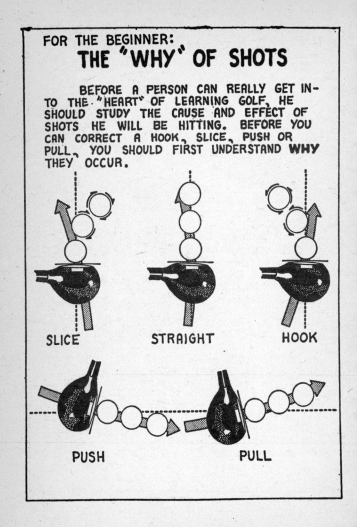

SLICE   STRAIGHT   HOOK

PUSH   PULL

STARTING THE DOWNSWING

"HITTING FROM THE TOP" BECOMES A PET-PEEVE TO MANY GOLFERS ON THE PRACTICE TEE AS THEY STRIVE TO ACKNOWLEDGE THEIR INSTRUCTOR'S LESSON.

THIS UNHAPPY AILMENT CAN BE REMEDIED BY STARTING THE DOWNSWING WITH A WEIGHT SHIFT AND HIP TURN TO THE LEFT....WITH THE CLUBHEAD LAGGING BEHIND. TRY NOT TO FEEL ANY FLIPPING, OR "FLY-CASTING," OF THE CLUB AT THIS POINT.... AND NO DROPPING OF THE HANDS. THE ENTIRE ACTION MUST BE SMOOTH AND FIRM.

FOR THE BEGINNER:
ABOUT THE DOWNSWING

THE "STORED UP TENSION" BETWEEN THE HIPS AND SHOULDERS ON THE BACKSWING IS HEIGHTENED WHEN YOU BEGIN YOUR DOWNSWING BY **TURNING YOUR HIPS TO THE LEFT.** IT IS A COMBINATION OF (A) LATERAL AND (B) ROTATION SHIFT THAT CONTINUES IN UNISON, AS IT UNWINDS THE UPPER PART OF THE BODY. THIS CREATES EARLY SPEED AND TRANSFERS YOUR WEIGHT FROM THE RIGHT FOOT TO THE LEFT... TAKING YOUR HIPS OUT OF THE WAY AND GIVING YOUR ARMS PLENTY OF ROOM TO PASS. IT PUTS YOU IN A STRONG HITTING POSITION.. AS YOUR SHOULDERS, ARMS, AND HANDS WILL BE PROPERLY DELAYED SO THAT THEY CAN PRODUCE MAXIMUM PERFORMANCE AT THE RIGHT TIME.

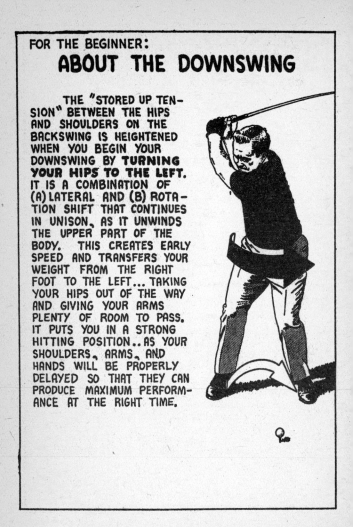

A GOOD START EQUALS A GOOD ENDING

THE VERY FIRST PART OF THE BACKSWING CAN DETERMINE THE SUCCESS OF THE ENTIRE SWING, SO A FEW "AUTOMATICS" SHOULD BE GROOVED DURING PRACTICE:

(1) TAKE THE CLUB STRAIGHT BACK FOR AS LONG AS THE TURNING OF THE HIPS AND SHOULDERS WILL ALLOW (THAT "INSIDE TRACK" RESTRICTS A LONG SWING ARC)

(2) TRY TO KEEP THE CLUBFACE SQUARE TO THE TARGET LINE

(3) MAINTAIN THE CONTINUATION OF LEFT ARM AND CLUBSHAFT TO INSURE A LATE WRIST-COCK

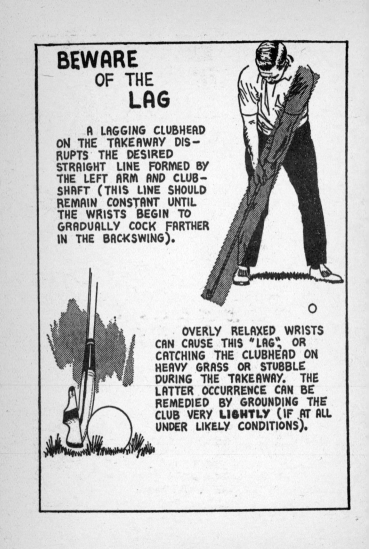

BEWARE
OF THE
LAG

A LAGGING CLUBHEAD ON THE TAKEAWAY DISRUPTS THE DESIRED STRAIGHT LINE FORMED BY THE LEFT ARM AND CLUBSHAFT (THIS LINE SHOULD REMAIN CONSTANT UNTIL THE WRISTS BEGIN TO GRADUALLY COCK FARTHER IN THE BACKSWING).

OVERLY RELAXED WRISTS CAN CAUSE THIS "LAG", OR CATCHING THE CLUBHEAD ON HEAVY GRASS OR STUBBLE DURING THE TAKEAWAY. THE LATTER OCCURRENCE CAN BE REMEDIED BY GROUNDING THE CLUB VERY **LIGHTLY** (IF AT ALL UNDER LIKELY CONDITIONS).

KEEPING AN EVEN TEMPO

TEMPO, OR RHYTHM, VARIES WITH THE IN-DIVIDUAL ... BUT WHETHER YOURS IS FAST, SLOW, OR MEDIUM, TRY TO KEEP THE TEMPO OF THE DOWNSWING IDENTI-CAL TO THAT OF THE BACKSWING.

THE COMBINATION OF A <u>SLOW</u> BACKSWING AND A <u>FAST</u> DOWNSWING SHOULD BE AVOIDED. ON THE DOWNSWING THE CLUBHEAD WILL AUTO-MATICALLY MOVE FASTER, BUT THE ARMS SHOULD MOVE AT THE APPROXIMATE SAME RATE OF SPEED AS ON THE BACKSWING.

POINTING AT THE TARGET

AT THE TOP OF THE BACKSWING YOUR CLUBSHAFT SHOULD POINT IN A STRAIGHT LINE DIRECTION TOWARD THE TARGET, WHETHER YOU TAKE THE CLUB TO "PARALLEL" OR, AS I DO, SHORT OF PARALLEL.

THE PURPOSE IS TO MAINTAIN A RECIPROCATING STRAIGHT-LINE MOTION TO THE ARC THROUGH-OUT THE SWING.

IF THE SHAFT POINTS EITHER <u>LEFT</u> OR <u>RIGHT</u> OF THE TARGET, THE ENTIRE ARC BECOMES ALTER-ED... USUALLY RE-SULTING IN AN ERRATIC SHOT.

FOR THE BEGINNER:
SWING TOWARD YOUR TARGET

IN YOUR BASIC SWING DEVELOPMENT TRY TO MAKE THE CLUBHEAD TRAVEL RIGHT TOWARD THE TARGET. THE SWING SHOULD PARALLEL AS NEARLY AS POSSIBLE THE "LINE OF FLIGHT", SO THAT IF YOU WERE TO LET GO OF THE CLUB AFTER IMPACT, IT WOULD FLY STRAIGHT AT THE TARGET.

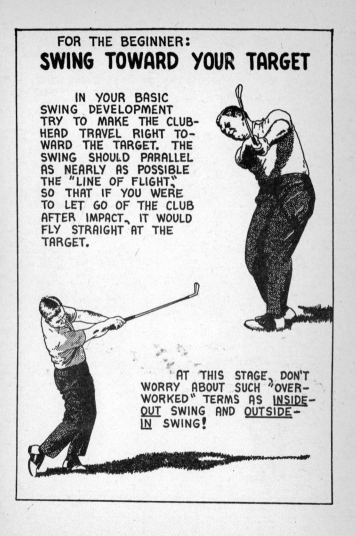

AT THIS STAGE, DON'T WORRY ABOUT SUCH "OVERWORKED" TERMS AS <u>INSIDE-OUT</u> SWING AND <u>OUTSIDE-IN</u> SWING!

HIT AGAINST A FIRM LEFT SIDE

TOO MANY GOLFERS LET THEIR LEFT SIDES "CRUMBLE" IN THE HITTING ZONE. THIS REALLY ROBS THEIR **POWER**.

TRY TO HIT AGAINST A FIRM LEFT SIDE!

WHEN I COME IN TO THE BALL I HAVE A FEELING OF EXTENDING THE WHOLE LEFT SIDE OF MY BODY AND THEREBY KEEPING THE RIGHT SIDE DOWN AND "UNDER" THE BALL FOR POWER. I TRY TO RETAIN THIS FIRMNESS IN MY LEFT SIDE AND LEFT LEG FOR AS LONG AS POSSIBLE.

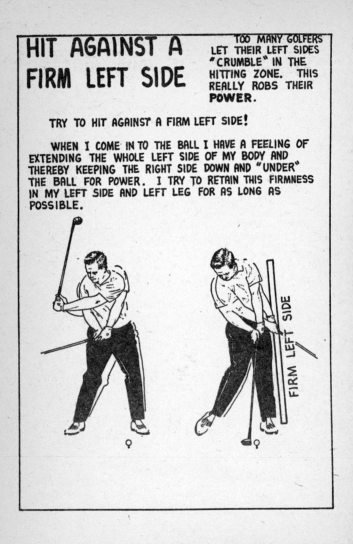

FIRM LEFT SIDE

FOR THE BEGINNER:
MAINTAIN A FIRM LEFT ARM

FULL ARM EXTENSION THROUGH THE BALL IS ESSENTIAL... REGARDLESS OF CLUB BEING USED. THIS IS USUALLY RELATIVELY EASY TO ACCOMPLISH WITH THE SWEEPING SWING OF THE WOODS-- ESPECIALLY THE DRIVER-- BUT REQUIRES SPECIAL CONCENTRATION WITH THE IRONS--ESPECIALLY THE <u>SHORT IRONS</u>.

BECAUSE OF THE SHORT IRONS' SHARPER DESCENT IN TO THE BALL, ANY BREAKING OF THE LEFT ARM <u>SHORTENS</u> THE SWING ARC AND CREATES A TENDENCY TO DIG. SO PAY PARTICULAR ATTENTION TO MAINTAINING A STRAIGHT LEFT ARM UNTIL WELL AFTER IMPACT... WITH **ALL** CLUBS!

MAINTAIN A LEVEL HEAD

HEAD POSITION IS ONE OF THE MOST IMPORTANT ASPECTS IN GOLF. YOUR HEAD MUST REMAIN ABSOLUTELY **LEVEL** DURING THE SWING. IT MUST NOT MOVE BACK OR FORTH, NEITHER MUST IT MOVE UP OR DOWN. BOBBING THE HEAD DISRUPTS THE WHOLE SWING AND MAKES CONTROL AND SOLID CONTACT ALMOST IMPOSSIBLE.

BE ESPECIALLY CAREFUL NOT TO DROP YOUR HEAD ON THE BACKSWING (THEN KEEPING IT ON THE SAME PLANE UNTIL AFTER IMPACT).

A LEVEL HEAD PROMOTES A LEVEL BODY, A LEVEL SWING, AND A SOLID HIT.

A SIMPLE CHECKPOINT ON
PUSHING OR PULLING

THE NEXT TIME SOME OF YOUR SHOTS GO ASTRAY, LEFT OR RIGHT... TRY THIS CHECKPOINT (THAT ISN'T REALLY AS TOUGH TO **DO** AS IT MAY SOUND):

VISUALIZE THE IMAGINARY PATH ALONG WHICH YOU TOOK THE CLUBHEAD BACK, AND THEN TRY TO MAKE THE CLUB RETURN TO THE BALL ALONG THE SAME PLANE...

I BELIEVE THIS WILL HELP SET UP THAT "SQUARE" HIT.

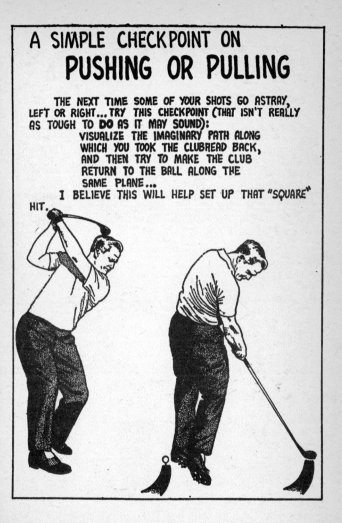

STAYING DOWN
WITH THE SHOT

ANXIETY CAUSES MANY GOLFERS TO PULL UP TOO QUICKLY AFTER HITTING THE BALL... CAUSING AN INCONSISTENT "FLICKING" ACTION WHICH RESULTS IN OFF-LINE SHOTS.

PRACTICE STAYING DOWN LONGER WITH THE SHOT BY KEEPING YOUR FOLLOWTHROUGH **LOW.** EXTEND BOTH ARMS AS FAR AS POSSIBLE AFTER THE HIT. THIS GREATER EXTENSION SEEMS TO ALLOW THE BALL TO REMAIN ON THE CLUBFACE LONGER, WHICH INCREASES YOUR CHANCES FOR A STRAIGHT SHOT.

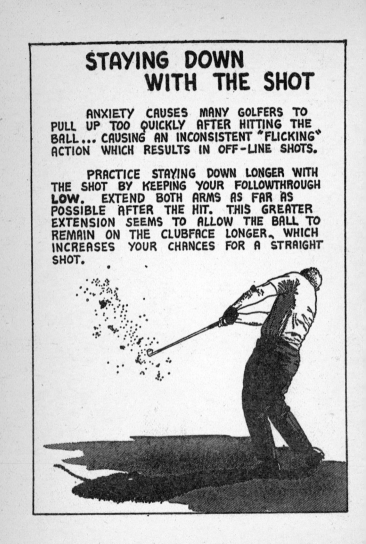

BE CAREFUL OF HASTY CHANGES

COUNTLESS GOLFERS, UPON FINDING THEIR SHOTS GOING ASTRAY, IMMEDIATELY BEGIN TO FIDDLE AROUND WITH THE GRIP, STANCE, ETC., WHEN OFTEN THE FAULT LIES ELSEWHERE. TWO WRONGS DO NOT MAKE A RIGHT.... SO TRY TO LOCATE THE TROUBLE BEFORE YOU MAKE SOME HASTY ADJUSTMENTS.

BEGIN YOUR SWING CHECK WITH THE BASICS. IF YOU FIND THE GRIP AND STANCE IN ORDER, THEN CHECK YOUR BACK-SWING, HEAD POSITION, FOOT ACTION, WEIGHT SHIFT, ETC.

REMEMBER THAT TOO MANY EXPERIMENT-AL CHANGES WILL OFTEN DESTROY WHAT WAS ALREADY SOUND IN YOUR SWING!

ROLE OF THE TEE SHOT

BEING A LONG HITTER IS A GREAT ADVANTAGE FACTOR IN GOLF, BUT ALWAYS REMEMBER THAT DISTANCE IS **ONLY** A FACTOR. THE TEE SHOT IS SOLELY AN EFFORT TO PLACE THE BALL IN POSITION FOR THE SECOND SHOT, AND **NEARNESS** TO THE HOLE IS NOT ALWAYS THE "BEST" POSITION.

SO DON'T JUST WHACK AWAY...PLAY FOR POSITION. YOU ARE PLAYING A GOLF HOLE, NOT PARTICIPATING IN A DRIVING CONTEST.

FOR THE BEGINNER:
ALL CLUBS SHOULD SWING ALIKE

EVEN THOUGH THE WEDGE AND SHORT IRONS DEMAND MORE UPRIGHT SWINGS.... BASICALLY SPEAKING, THE SAME SWING CAN BE APPLIED FOR **ALL** CLUBS. THE PLANE NECESSARILY CHANGES FROM THE WEDGE THROUGH THE DRIVER AS SHAFT LENGTH DICTATES DISTANCE FROM THE BALL, BUT EVERY (NORMAL) SHOT IS PLAYED OFF THE LEFT HEEL WITH THE SAME CONSTANT SWING.

THE ONLY DIFFERING ASPECTS ARE THAT YOU HIT **DOWN** SLIGHTLY MORE WITH THE IRONS, AND THAT THE BALL IS HIT SLIGHTLY ON THE UPSWING WITH THE DRIVER.

FOR THE BEGINNER:
SHAFT FLEX
AND
SWING WEIGHT

HEAVY CLUBHEAD WITH STIFF SHAFT

IN RESPECT TO SWING WEIGHT, LENGTH, AND FLEX OF SHAFT—SELECTION OF A SET OF CLUBS IS LARGELY A MATTER OF PERSONAL PREFERENCE. HOWEVER, **WEIGHT** AND **FLEX** SHOULD HARMONIZE.

A LARGE, STRONG GOLFER USUALLY PREFERS A LONGER THAN AVERAGE DRIVER WITH A HEAVY CLUBHEAD. HE SHOULD HAVE A STIFF (X) SHAFT TO COUNTERBALANCE THE HEAVY HEAD. DESPITE BEING CONSIDERED A STRONG HITTER, I PERSONALLY PREFER A REGULAR LENGTH DRIVER (43"), AND A LIGHT HEAD (D-1) WITH AN S SHAFT (WHICH IS A LITTLE WHIPPIER THAN AN X — BUT REACTS LIKE ONE SINCE THE SWING WEIGHT IS SO LIGHT).

SO WHATEVER LENGTH SHAFT YOU CHOOSE TO MATCH YOUR PHYSIQUE, ALSO **MATCH** WEIGHT AND FLEX.

MEDIUM-STIFF SHAFT WITH LIGHT HEAD

CHOICE OF BALL

THE EXTENT THAT A GOLFER COMPRESSES A GOLF BALL SHOULD DICTATE HIS PREFERENCE IN CHOOSING THE "RIGHT" BALL TO FIT HIS SWING.

A "HARD" SWINGER WILL OBTAIN BEST RESULTS FROM USING A HIGH COMPRESSION BALL (85 UP) BECAUSE HE TENDS TO **OVER**-COMPRESS A MEDIUM BALL (70 TO 85). THE AVERAGE HITTER USUALLY IS UNABLE TO COMPRESS A TIGHTLY WOUND HARD BALL, AND THUS SHOULD USE THE MEDIUM BALL TO FIT HIS SWING. (FOR A VERY EASY SWING, A "LOW" COMPRESSION BALL -- 70 OR UNDER -- MAY PROVE BEST.)

WHY NOT A FIVE-WOOD?

IF YOU HAVE REACHED THE POINT OF DISGUST WITH YOUR LONG-IRON PLAY, IT MIGHT BE ADVISABLE TO CARRY A FIVE-WOOD. THIS CLUB WILL GET THE BALL IN THE AIR FASTER AND BRING IT DOWN MORE SOFTLY THAN A TWO-IRON. THE ADDED LOFT OF THE FIVE-WOOD SHOULD GIVE YOU ADDITIONAL CONFIDENCE.

AND DON'T WORRY ABOUT THAT **PRIDE**......I KNOW SOME PROFESSIONALS WHO USE FIVE-WOODS!

5 WOOD

2 IRON

CHAPTER 4
Make Your Long Game Longer

There is no part of the game that precipitates more eager-
ness and produces greater frustration than trying for extra
length, whether it's off the tee or back on the fairway. On
occasion, the average golfer can easily delude himself into
thinking he can hit the ball farther and straighter than he
really can, with the result that in trying to prove it, he often
winds up hitting neither his longest nor his most accurate
shot.

Reaching for those extra yards, all of us are subject to
a variety of technical errors—anything from hitting from
the top to shanking. Now, the average golfer who has had
instruction from a professional is well aware of all the
things that can go wrong when he tries to overpower the
ball. But the temptation to do so is always there, and this
causes him to lose his concentration and consequently his
form.

This is when it's most important to remember that you
don't attain more distance by overswinging. Distance is
gained by building up club-head speed, not by swinging
harder. Once you upset the natural rhythm of your swing,
you destroy the very foundation of your game. Never allow
yourself to lose that precious mechanism of timing—not
for all the 300-yard drives in your bag.

There are many ways to add yards to your drives. One
of them is to take a higher backswing by bringing your
hands more to the top. This immediately increases the arc
of your swing and will enable you to get into the ball with
greater impact, thereby delivering a longer, but controlled,
hit. But none of this works if you aren't using your legs
properly and transferring your weight correctly. Here, in
this section, are my recommended methods for hitting the
ball farther than you have in the past. But you'll see that it
takes as much willpower as raw power to apply them to
your own game.

TRY TO HIT SOME WARM-UP SHOTS

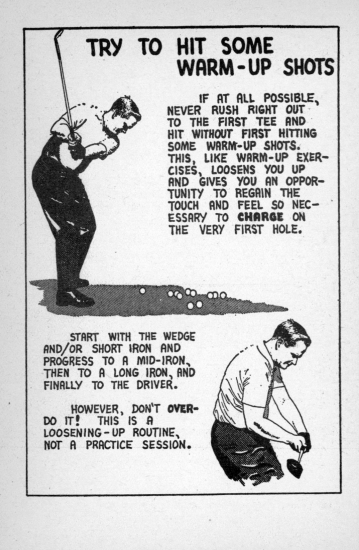

IF AT ALL POSSIBLE, NEVER RUSH RIGHT OUT TO THE FIRST TEE AND HIT WITHOUT FIRST HITTING SOME WARM-UP SHOTS. THIS, LIKE WARM-UP EXERCISES, LOOSENS YOU UP AND GIVES YOU AN OPPORTUNITY TO REGAIN THE TOUCH AND FEEL SO NECESSARY TO **CHARGE** ON THE VERY FIRST HOLE.

START WITH THE WEDGE AND/OR SHORT IRON AND PROGRESS TO A MID-IRON, THEN TO A LONG IRON, AND FINALLY TO THE DRIVER.

HOWEVER, DON'T **OVER**-DO IT! THIS IS A LOOSENING-UP ROUTINE, NOT A PRACTICE SESSION.

SWING *HIGHER* FOR EXTRA YARDAGE

EVERY GOLFER OCCASIONALLY FEELS IT'S TIME TO "LET OUT THE SHAFT"..! THE RESULT IS USUALLY AN EXCESSIVE PIVOT, A LUNGE AT THE BALL ..... AND **LESS** DISTANCE.

IF YOU WILL TAKE YOUR HANDS **HIGHER** AT THE TOP YOU WILL INCREASE YOUR SWING ARC .... HENCEFORTH ENABLING YOU TO INCREASE THE MOMENTUM OF THE DOWNSWING.

I TRY TO ALWAYS HAVE MY HANDS ABOVE MY SHOULDERS AT THE TOP .... IF NOT ABOVE MY HEAD!

EXTEND 'BOTH' ARMS AFTER IMPACT

SINCE I FAVOR A FADE FOR A MAJORITY OF MY SHOTS I NEVER WANT MY HANDS TO TURN OVER AFTER IMPACT UNTIL THEY ABSOLUTELY MUST.

THUS, I TRY TO KEEP BOTH ARMS EXTENDED AS LONG AS I POSSIBLY CAN **AFTER IMPACT**. THIS ASSURES ME THAT I HAVE CLEARED MY LEFT SIDE AND BROUGHT MY RIGHT KNEE THROUGH, WHILE CHECKING THE PREMATURE ROLLING OF MY WRISTS.

IMPORTANCE
OF THE
DRIVE

THE WELL-WORN MAXIM OF "YOU DRIVE FOR SHOW AND PUTT FOR DOUGH" HAS AN ELEMENT OF TRUTH, BUT DON'T TAKE IT TOO LITERALLY. THE DRIVE IS THE OPENING MANEUVER IN YOUR ATTACK ON A HOLE. IT'S LIKE THE OPENING LEAD IN A BRIDGE HAND, OR THE FIRST PLAY A QUARTER-BACK CALLS IN A SERIES OF DOWNS. A GOOD "BEGINNING" JUST CANNOT BE OVER-EMPHASIZED!

A GOOD DRIVE OPENS UP A HOLE TO A PAR OR BIRDIE; A CARELESS DRIVE PUTS YOU IN A POSITION FROM WHICH YOU MIGHT HAVE TO SALVAGE A BOGEY. SO THE PROPER PLACE TO START BEARING DOWN IS RIGHT ON THE TEE!

LEG ACTION IN THE BACKSWING

AS I START MY BACK-SWING I CONSCIOUSLY SHIFT MY WEIGHT IMMEDIATELY TO THE **INSIDE** OF MY RIGHT FOOT. AS A MATTER OF FACT, I FEEL THAT THIS IS ACTUALLY THE **INITIAL** ACTION IN MY BACKSWING.

WITH WEIGHT ON THE INSIDE OF THE RIGHT FOOT, I FEEL THAT MY RIGHT KNEE IS STEADY--ALMOST LOCKED INTO POSITION. THIS KEEPS MY BODY **TURNING** IN-STEAD OF SWAYING LATER-ALLY TO THE RIGHT AND "OFF THE BALL."

USING YOUR LEGS FOR POWER

MAXIMUM SWING POWER IS POSSIBLE ONLY THROUGH PROPER LEG ACTION.

AS THE DOWNSWING BEGINS, THE LEGS ASSIST THE HIP-TURN AND WEIGHT-SHIFT TO THE LEFT. ABOUT HALFWAY DOWN THE LEGS <u>REALLY</u> COME INTO FULL PLAY, GENERATING A POWERFUL THRUST THAT PUSHES THE ARMS AND HIPS THROUGH TO THE FINISH.

WHEN TO LEAVE THE DRIVER IN THE BAG

WHEN FACED WITH THE PROBLEM OF WHETHER TO FORGET THE DRIVER AND SACRIFICE DISTANCE FOR ACCURACY, ASK YOURSELF THIS QUESTION:

IS THE POSSIBLE REWARD FOR ADDED DISTANCE WORTH THE RISK I MUST TAKE TO GET IT?

DRIVING DISTANCE

FAIRWAY WOOD—LONG IRON DISTANCE

WHEN THE FAIRWAY NARROWS OR TRAPS LOOM IN YOUR "DRIVING RANGE," PERCENTAGES FAVOR A FAIRWAY WOOD OR MAYBE EVEN AN IRON. REMEMBER... THE WEDGE SHOT TO THE GREEN WOULD HAVE BEEN WONDERFUL, BUT A SEVEN IRON APPROACH IS MUCH BETTER THAN ROLLING YOUR SECOND SHOT OUT OF THE TREES FOR A "THIRD" SHOT APPROACH.

USE A MAXIMUM
SHOULDER TURN

MANY GOLFERS MIS-
INTERPRET TODAY'S "COM-
PACT SWING" THEORY TO
SIGNIFY A SHORTER SWING
....AND, INVARIABLY, LESS
TURN.

A SMOOTH, COMPACT
SWING STILL REQUIRES A
FULL SHOULDER TURN.
TRY TO BE CONSCIOUS
OF A FULL TURN WHILE
PRACTICING UNTIL IT
BECOMES SECOND NATURE.

(A "FIVE O'CLOCK SHADOW"
CHECK IS ONE TEST TO
DETERMINE IF YOUR
SHOULDER CONSISTENTLY
REACHES UNDER YOUR
CHIN, BECAUSE IT WILL
LITERALLY START WEAR-
ING A HOLE IN YOUR
SHIRT AT THE SHOULDER)

DON'T PAUSE AT THE TOP

I DON'T BELIEVE IN A PAUSE AT THE TOP OF THE BACKSWING BECAUSE IT DESTROYS THE FLOWING, UNINTERRUPTED MOTION OF THE SWING.

JUST BEFORE THE CLUB REACHES THE PEAK OF THE BACKSWING, THE HIPS START THEIR TURN TO THE **LEFT**, AND THE ARMS AND HANDS LAG, BUT DO NOT PAUSE. THE HIPS THEN PULL THE LEFT ARM DOWN AND BRING THE CLUBHEAD THROUGH THE BALL (THIS IS WHAT PRODUCES **POWER**).

THE LEFT HAND AT THE TOP

THE POSITION YOUR LEFT HAND ATTAINS AT THE TOP OF THE BACKSWING CAN DICTATE THE KIND OF SHOT FORTHCOMING.

I TRY TO KEEP MY LEFTHAND IN THE SQUARE (OR STRAIGHT) POSITION, OR MAYBE SLIGHTLY OPEN. THE LATTER ENCOURAGES A FADE. I NEVER WANT IT "CLOSED" FOR FEAR OF A RESULTING HOOK OR EVEN A SMOTHERED SHOT.

STRAIGHT   OPEN   CLOSED

ABOUT THAT HIGH ELBOW

THE OLD SCHOOL OF THOUGHT THEORIZES THE RIGHT ELBOW TO <u>NEVER</u> LEAVE THE SIDE ON THE BACKSWING. EVEN THOUGH I AM NOT CONSCIOUS OF IT DURING MY SWING--I AM FULLY AWARE THAT MY RIGHT ELBOW DOES MOVE AWAY FROM MY BODY.

BUT I FEEL THAT THIS POSITION DEFINITELY PROVIDES A WIDER SWING ARC. (ON THE DOWNSWING THE ELBOW NECESSARILY RETURNS TO MY RIGHT SIDE WITHOUT CONSCIOUS DIRECTION ON MY PART.)

WEIGHT DISTRIBUTION AT THE TOP،

TRY TO CONCENTRATE ON KEEPING YOUR WEIGHT BASICALLY ON THE <u>INSIDE</u> OF THE FEET FROM ADDRESS TO THE VERY PEAK OF YOUR BACK-SWING.

AT THE TOP 85% TO 90% OF YOUR WEIGHT SHOULD HAVE SHIFTED TO THE **INSIDE** OF THE **RIGHT FOOT**... THE REMAINDER STILL CARRIED BY THE INSIDE OF THE LEFT. THIS KEEPS THE BODY CENTERED AND PROPER HIP TURN CAN BE PERFORMED WITHOUT SWAY-ING.

KEEP YOUR
HEAD
DOWN

COMING OFF THE BALL, OR PULLING UP, IS A COMMON PROBLEM THAT CAN BE SOLVED THROUGH AN EXAGGERATED EFFORT TO KEEP YOUR HEAD FROM COMING UP AFTER THE HIT.

WHEN PRACTICING, TRY TO COMPLETELY FINISH THE SWING WITHOUT LIFTING YOUR HEAD.. WHILE KEEPING YOUR EYES ON THE ORIGINAL BALL LOCATION. WHEN YOU RESUME YOUR NORMAL SWING FOLLOWING SUCH A PRACTICE SESSION, YOU WILL FIND IT EASIER FOR YOUR HEAD AND BODY TO HOLD "POSITION"... AND NOT UNTIL WELL AFTER IMPACT WILL THE HEAD RISE.

WEIGHT DISTRIBUTION
DOWN AND THROUGH

AS YOUR WEIGHT SHIFTS "LEFT" ON THE DOWNSWING, PRESSURE SHOULD REMAIN **INSIDE** BOTH FEET. JUST BEFORE IMPACT YOU SHOULD FEEL THAT THE MAJORITY OF YOUR WEIGHT IS ON THE **LEFT** FOOT.

TRY NOT TO LET YOUR WEIGHT GO FROM THE INSIDE TO THE OUTSIDE OF THE LEFT FOOT UNTIL YOU ARE 2 OR 3 FEET **THROUGH** THE BALL. AN EARLY SHIFT TO THE OUTSIDE MIGHT MOVE YOU OUT BEYOND THE BALL.

AT THE FINISH 95% OF YOUR WEIGHT SHOULD BE ON YOUR LEFT FOOT.

TRY "SWEEPING" THE LONG IRONS

THE MAJORITY OF GOLFERS WHO MIS-HIT THE LONG IRONS MAKE THE MISTAKE OF HITTING <u>DOWN</u> TOO MUCH ON THE SHOT. OFTEN, IN THEIR ATTEMPT TO GET A DIVOT, THEY HIT "FAT" BEHIND THE BALL.

TRY TO **SWEEP** THE BALL WITH A LONG IRON... KEEPING THE CLUBHEAD **LOW** AT IMPACT SO IT STRIKES THE BACK OF THE BALL SOLIDLY AND CONTINUES THROUGH WITHOUT CATCHING TURF. THE RESULT WILL BE MORE SATISFYING AND WITH GREATER CONSISTENCY.

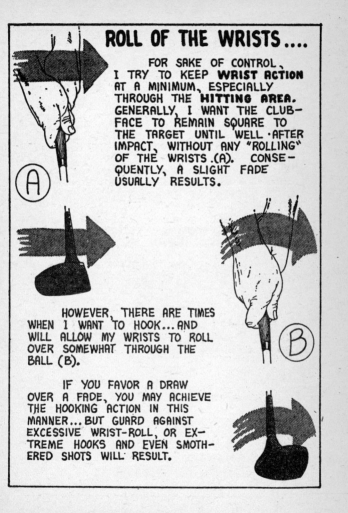

ROLL OF THE WRISTS....

FOR SAKE OF CONTROL, I TRY TO KEEP **WRIST ACTION** AT A MINIMUM, ESPECIALLY THROUGH THE **HITTING AREA.** GENERALLY, I WANT THE CLUB-FACE TO REMAIN SQUARE TO THE TARGET UNTIL WELL ·AFTER IMPACT, WITHOUT ANY "ROLLING" OF THE WRISTS .(A). CONSE-QUENTLY, A SLIGHT FADE USUALLY RESULTS.

HOWEVER, THERE ARE TIMES WHEN I WANT TO HOOK... AND WILL ALLOW MY WRISTS TO ROLL OVER SOMEWHAT THROUGH THE BALL (B).

IF YOU FAVOR A DRAW OVER A FADE, YOU MAY ACHIEVE THE HOOKING ACTION IN THIS MANNER... BUT GUARD AGAINST EXCESSIVE WRIST-ROLL, OR EX-TREME HOOKS AND EVEN SMOTH-ERED SHOTS WILL· RESULT.

KNEE BEND

HOW MUCH A GOLFER BENDS HIS KNEES DEPENDS ON PERSONAL PREFERENCE, JUST SO HE <u>DOES</u> FLEX THEM SOMEWHAT. HOWEVER, THERE ARE "RULES" OF LIMITATION.

DON'T HAVE THE KNEES SO SAGGY THAT THEY FLOP AROUND AS YOU SWING. THEY SHOULD STAY PRETTY MUCH IN THE SAME PLACE THROUGHOUT. ON THE OTHER HAND, STIFF LEGS ARE TABOO. THEY TEND TO MAKE YOU TENSE, LOCK THE BODY, AND RESTRICT THE TURN -- THUS ROBBING THE SWING OF POWER AND FLUIDITY.

GET A COMFORTABLE DEGREE OF KNEE BEND -- ONE WHICH IS FIRM, BUT FLEXIBLE.

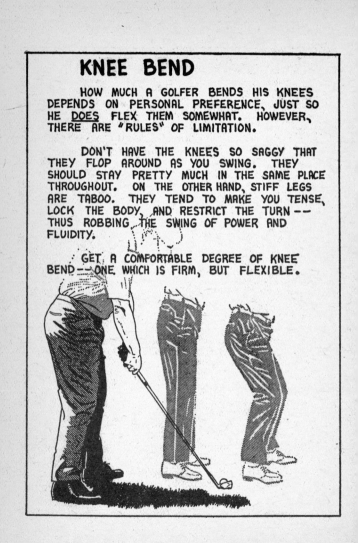

THE "HIGH" LONG IRON FROM THE TEE

WHEN IT IS DESIRABLE TO HIT A LONG IRON FROM THE TEE WITH AS MUCH HEIGHT AND CARRY AS POSSIBLE, **TEE THE BALL HIGH.**

DON'T TRY TO TAKE A DIVOT AFTER HITTING THE BALL (AS YOU GENERALLY MIGHT DO WHEN TEEING THE BALL LOW). THE IDEA HERE IS TO STRIKE THE BALL SOLIDLY AT THE BOTTOM OF THE SWING WITH A **SWEEPING MOTION.**

DRIVING TO A SOFT FAIRWAY

HOW DOES ONE ACHIEVE MAXIMUM DISTANCE WHEN DRIVING TO A SOFT FAIRWAY? A LOW HOOK IS THE CHOICE OF SOME GOLFERS, BUT I PREFER A **HIGH** HOOK OR **HIGH** FADE -- TO GET AS MUCH <u>CARRY</u> AS POSSIBLE.

PERSONALLY, I FIND THAT A HIGH <u>FADE</u> GIVES ME GREATEST DISTANCE WHEN THERE IS NO WIND. I TEE THE BALL HIGH AND FARTHER FORWARD IN MY STANCE, AND TRY TO KEEP MY RIGHT SHOULDER **DOWN** AND **UNDER** IN THE HITTING AREA... WITH A PRONOUNCED EXTENSION OF MY ARMS AS FAR AS POSSIBLE AFTER IMPACT.

12

ABOUT
THE
FOLLOW-THROUGH

THE SO-CALLED "PICTURE" FINISH IS MERELY A NATURAL CONTINUATION OF THE FOLLOW-THROUGH.

I AM MORE OR LESS THROUGH "HITTING THE BALL" (WITH A DRIVER) WHEN THE CLUB REACHES A ONE OR TWO O'CLOCK POSITION... WHICH ACTUALLY ENDS THE FOLLOW-THROUGH. THE LENGTH OF THE CLUB USUALLY DICTATES THE EXTENT OF THE FOLLOW-THROUGH. JUST BE SURE YOU FEEL THAT YOU'RE STILL FIRMLY "POWERING" THE SHOT UNTIL THE FINISH OF THE SWING.

CHAPTER 5

Finessing the Ball

At least once in every round of golf you are bound to run into a golfing problem you feel you aren't quite up to. A sudden gust will disturb a player who doesn't know how to play the wind. A golfer who doesn't know how to control his ball coming out of the rough will find himself imbedded in a cabbage patch. Here high- and low-handicap golfers alike have something in common: both approach the shot with a good deal of trepidation.

There is no need to allow such problems to turn a promising round into a disastrous one. While there are universally accepted ways of playing conventional shots, there are also proven methods of licking such out-of-the-ordinary ones as hitting out of a divot, off wet, slick turf, or from sand in the rough. These represent finesse shots, which require a certain amount of trial and error, in addition to plenty of practice.

I've therefore loaded this section with as many examples of trouble shots as you are likely to encounter in an entire season. The important thing is not to get discouraged when you find yourself in unexpected trouble and doubt that you have the right shot in your bag. Many golfers beat themselves the moment they find their ball in an uncomfortable position; they immediately anticipate disaster and they usually find it.

But to tell you the truth, I have seen just as many rounds saved by a great recovery shot as those that were ruined by a negative attitude. You have to think positively in all circumstances. But it also helps if you know what you're doing.

TEE IT NORMAL IN A HEADWIND

MANY PLAYERS ADVISE TEEING THE BALL <u>LOW</u> FOR A DRIVE INTO THE WIND. FOR AVERAGE GOLFERS I FEEL THAT THE BALL SHOULD BE HIGH ENOUGH TO GET ALL OF THE CLUBFACE ON THE BALL; AFTER ALL, THIS IS ONE SITUATION THAT REALLY DEMANDS A **SOLID** HIT.

TEEING THE BALL LOW WILL TEND TO PRODUCE A MORE DOWNWARD BLOW RATHER THAN A "SWEEP", AND THE DOWNWARD BLOW WILL PRODUCE THE GREATER AMOUNT OF SPIN.

A SLICE MIGHT OCCUR ALSO WITH THE BALL TEED LOW, BECAUSE MOST PLAYERS WILL OPEN THE FACE OF THE CLUB AT IMPACT TO CONFORM TO THE TERRAIN (AS CUSTOMARILY HAPPENS WHEN A DRIVER IS USED FROM THE FAIRWAY).

THE INTENTIONAL HIGH SHOT

HOW OFTEN HAVE YOU DRIVEN INTO AN ADJACENT FAIRWAY AND HAD TO CONTINUE DOWN IT ON YOUR SECOND SHOT FOR FEAR OF NOT CLEARING THE INTERVENING TREES? I'M SURE THAT A WELL-EXECUTED "HIGH SHOT" WOULD HAVE SAVED A STROKE OR TWO.

THE <u>INTENTIONAL HIGH SHOT</u> SHOULD BE IN YOUR REPERTOIRE OF SHOTS.

BALL POSITIONING IS A CHIEF FACTOR ON THIS SHOT. PLAY IT FORWARD OFF THE LEFT TOE AND OPEN THE CLUBFACE SLIGHTLY. BE SURE **NOT** TO ROLL THE HANDS AT IMPACT OR JUST AFTER.

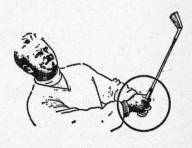

"TEE UP" ON PAR THREES

ALWAYS TEE THE BALL WHEN PLAYING PAR 3 HOLES. OTHERWISE, YOU RUN THE RISK OF GRASS COMING BETWEEN THE CLUBFACE AND THE BALL (WHICH CAN CAUSE SOME UNFAVORABLE RESULTS), OR OF NOT MAKING SOLID CONTACT.

I TEE THE BALL FAIRLY LOW, BUT HIGH ENOUGH TO AVOID THE GRASS PROBLEM AND IN A POSITION TO PROMOTE A **CLEAN** HIT.

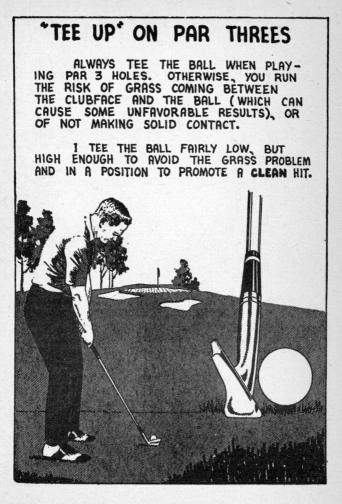

SWING UPRIGHT FOR BACKSPIN

IF YOU ARE HAVING TROUBLE ACHIEVING PROPER BITE WITH YOUR APPROACH SHOTS, YOUR SWING MAY BE TOO <u>FLAT</u>.

AN UPRIGHT SWING WILL BRING ABOUT MAXIMUM BACKSPIN BECAUSE IT ALLOWS THE CLUBHEAD TO COME INTO THE BALL AT A <u>STEEP</u> ANGLE WITH A **CUTTING** TYPE OF ACTION, WHEREAS A FLAT SWING WILL CAUSE THE BALL TO HOOK AND RUN WITH OVERSPIN.

ROLLING THE WRISTS TOO SOON AFTER IMPACT (WHICH USUALLY ACCOMPANIES A FLAT SWING) ENHANCES A HOOKING ACTION ALSO, SO TRY TO MOVE YOUR HANDS STRAIGHT OUT TOWARD THE TARGET!

AN ANGLE ON THE LEFT FOOT

45°

CONVENTIONAL

A "SMALL" STANCE ADJUSTMENT CAN PAY OFF IN **BIG** HITS! TRY OPENING YOUR LEFT TOE POSITION MORE THAN THE CONVENTIONAL ANGLE CALLS FOR.

I POSITION MINE AT ABOUT A 45° ANGLE TOWARD THE DIRECTION OF PLAY. THIS PERMITS ME TO COME THROUGH THE BALL WITH A COMPLETE UNCOILING OF MY LEFT SIDE, WITH A CONTINUOUS ACCELERATION OF THE CLUBHEAD.

NEGOTIATING THE *HIGH* SIDEHILL LIE

KEEPING YOUR BALANCE IS A **MUST** ON THIS SHOT SINCE THE BALL IS NEARER TO YOU THAN NORMAL, COUNTERBALANCE VIA A CHOKED GRIP AND AN UPRIGHT STANCE (WITH KNEES FLEXED ONLY SLIGHTLY AND WEIGHT NEARER YOUR TOES).

THIS SHOT TENDS TO HOOK, SO HIT IT TO THE RIGHT. TRY TO "SLOW DOWN" AND SWING MORE "COMPACT" THAN YOU NORMALLY DO. DO NOT TAKE A DIVOT (TRY TO "SWEEP" THE BALL RIGHT OFF THE TURF).

NEGOTIATING THE *LOW* SIDEHILL LIE

THIS RATHER HAZARDOUS SHOT CAN BE NEGOTIATED SUCCESSFULLY IF YOU WILL STAY DOWN ON IT WITH A <u>COMPACT</u> SWING.

BY GRIPPING THE CLUB AT THE END AND FLEXING THE KNEES SUFFICIENTLY YOU CAN SIMULATE THE DISTANCE FROM THE BALL AS FOR A NORMAL LIE. KEEP YOUR WEIGHT ON YOUR **HEELS!**

THIS SHOT FADES... SO AIM TO THE LEFT OF THE TARGET. USE A RATHER COMPACT SWING WITHOUT VARYING YOUR RHYTHM, AND STAY DOWN WITH THE SHOT ALL THE WAY THROUGH THE FINISH.

EXECUTING THE 'TRICKY' DOWNHILL SHOT

THIS SHOT IS TRICKY BE-CAUSE IT NOT ONLY INVOLVES MARKED SWING ADJUSTMENTS BUT ALSO A "BALANCE" ALTERA-TION. OPEN YOUR STANCE WITH MOST OF YOUR WEIGHT CARRIED ON THE **LEFT SIDE**. COME UP A CLUB (7 TO AN 8, ETC.) TO OFFSET THE LOW TRAJECTORY, AND PLAY THE BALL BACK MORE TOWARD THE RIGHT FOOT. OPEN THE CLUBFACE A LITTLE (TO OFFSET A PULLING TENDEN-CY) AND BREAK YOUR WRISTS QUICKLY ON THE BACKSWING. HIT THIS SHOT **HARD** AND KEEP THE WRISTS FROM ROLLING TOO SOON AFTER IMPACT!

HITTING FROM WET TURF

EVEN THOUGH SOME GOLFERS NEVER HAVE TO WORRY ABOUT HITTING FROM WET TURF, MOST ENTHUSIASTS WILL ENCOUNTER THE PROBLEM SOONER OR LATER.

MOISTURE FROM THE WET GRASS FILLS THE CLUBFACE GROOVES...WHICH MINIMIZES BACKSPIN. COUNTERACT THIS WITH A **FADE** INTO THE GREEN. MOVE UP A CLUB (5 TO 6, ETC.), AIM TO THE LEFT...AND WITH A PRONOUNCED **ARM** SWING... PICK THE BALL CLEANLY FROM THE TURF, DELAYING THE WRISTS' ROLL AFTER IMPACT.

HITTING OFF HARD PAN

PLAYING OFF OF HARD, UNBROKEN GROUND IS **ONE** SHOT IN WHICH YOU **MUST** RELY ON THE LOFT OF THE CLUB TO LIFT THE BALL.

TO PROPERLY "PINCH" THE BALL OFF HARDPAN I MAKE ONE MINOR ALTERATION IN MY SWING. I TRY TO CONSCIOUSLY KEEP MY HANDS WELL **AHEAD** OF THE BALL AT IMPACT. BY KEEPING WRIST ACTION TO A MINIMUM AND HITTING DOWN FIRMLY, I OFFSET ANY TENDENCY I MAY HAVE TO SCOOP THE BALL.

HITTING OUT
OF A DIVOT

THERE IS NO NEED TO PANIC WHEN CON-FRONTED WITH A "DIVOT LIE." THE SAFEST APPROACH IS THE **PUNCH SHOT.** SELECT A CLUB **ONE** LONGER THAN YOU ORDINARILY NEED (7 TO A 6, ETC.) AND PLAY THE BALL BACK TOWARD THE RIGHT FOOT (WITH YOUR HANDS REMAINING **AHEAD** OF THE BALL). USE A THREE-QUARTER SWING, PICK-ING THE CLUB UP ABRUPTLY, AND SWING DOWN ON TOP OF THE BALL.... KEEPING YOUR HANDS SQUARE TO THE TARGET <u>WELL AFTER IMPACT.</u> REMEMBER, THE TRAJECTORY WILL BE LOW AND THE BALL WILL RUN AFTER IT HITS.

HITTING OUT OF CLOVER

INVARIABLY A SHOT OUT OF CLOVER WILL RUN AFTER IT LANDS BECAUSE THE CLOVER GETS BETWEEN THE CLUBHEAD AND THE BALL -- ELIMINATING BACKSPIN.

WHEN FACED WITH ONE OF THESE "FLIER" LIES, TAKE ONE CLUB LESS TO ALLOW FOR THE ADDITIONAL RUN.... AND TRY TO SWING DOWN MORE WITH YOUR <u>HANDS</u> THAN USUAL. THIS TENDS TO UNCOCK THE WRISTS SOONER, ENABLING YOU TO COME INTO THE BALL AT A SHALLOWER LEVEL.

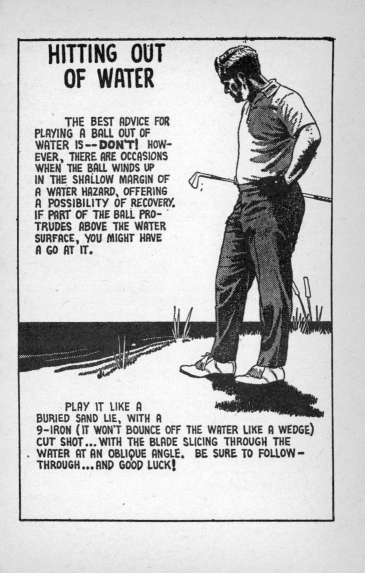

HITTING OUT
OF WATER

THE BEST ADVICE FOR PLAYING A BALL OUT OF WATER IS--**DON'T!** HOWEVER, THERE ARE OCCASIONS WHEN THE BALL WINDS UP IN THE SHALLOW MARGIN OF A WATER HAZARD, OFFERING A POSSIBILITY OF RECOVERY. IF PART OF THE BALL PROTRUDES ABOVE THE WATER SURFACE, YOU MIGHT HAVE A GO AT IT.

PLAY IT LIKE A BURIED SAND LIE, WITH A 9-IRON (IT WON'T BOUNCE OFF THE WATER LIKE A WEDGE) CUT SHOT...WITH THE BLADE SLICING THROUGH THE WATER AT AN OBLIQUE ANGLE. BE SURE TO FOLLOW-THROUGH...AND GOOD LUCK!

HITTING FROM SAND IN THE ROUGH

SEASIDE GOLFERS VERY FREQUENTLY ARE FACED WITH A SANDY LIE IN THE ROUGH. THIS SHOT IS UNLIKE THE HIT FROM GRASSY ROUGH... FOR THE LIE IS TIGHT WITH NO ROOM FOR THE CLUB TO CUT UNDERNEATH, AND THE SAND HAS LESS GIVE.

FIRMNESS

FIRM UP YOUR STANCE (ESPECIALLY IN LOOSE SAND) AND DON'T SWING TOO HARD. SELECT A LONGER CLUB THAN USUAL TO OFFSET A REDUCED BACKSWING, AND GRIP TIGHTER THAN USUAL WITH YOUR **LEFT HAND.** TAKE THE CLUB BACK A LITTLE MORE ABRUPTLY, PLAY THE BALL BACK NEAR THE CENTER TO INSURE HITTING IT FIRST, AND.....
FOLLOW THROUGH.

THE PINE STRAW "EXPLOSION"

I'M SURE THAT ALL GOLFERS WHO PLAY ON COURSES BLESSED WITH AN ABUNDANCE OF BEAUTIFUL PINES HAVE HIT SOME PECULIAR SHOTS OFF PINE STRAW!

THE NEXT TIME YOU'RE FACED WITH A "STRAW" LIE AND NEED TO GET THE BALL UP QUICKLY TO CLEAR SAND, BUSHES, WATER, ETC. .... TRY AN **EXPLOSION** SHOT.

USING A SAND OR PITCHING WEDGE, PICK UP THE CLUB QUICKLY AND WITH AN OPEN FACE.... AND COME DOWN ABOUT HALF-AN-INCH OR AN INCH BEHIND THE BALL, HITTING HARDER THAN FOR A NORMAL SHOT.

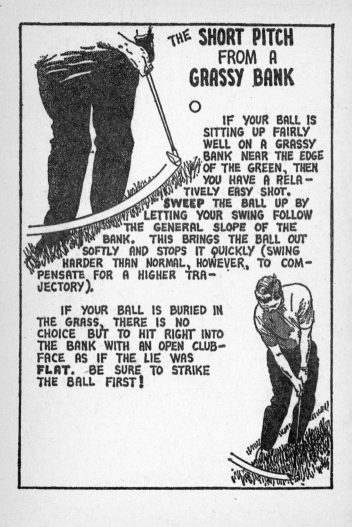

THE **SHORT PITCH** FROM A **GRASSY BANK**

IF YOUR BALL IS SITTING UP FAIRLY WELL ON A GRASSY BANK NEAR THE EDGE OF THE GREEN, THEN YOU HAVE A RELATIVELY EASY SHOT. SWEEP THE BALL UP BY LETTING YOUR SWING FOLLOW THE GENERAL SLOPE OF THE BANK. THIS BRINGS THE BALL OUT SOFTLY AND STOPS IT QUICKLY (SWING HARDER THAN NORMAL, HOWEVER, TO COMPENSATE FOR A HIGHER TRAJECTORY).

IF YOUR BALL IS BURIED IN THE GRASS, THERE IS NO CHOICE BUT TO HIT RIGHT INTO THE BANK WITH AN OPEN CLUBFACE AS IF THE LIE WAS FLAT. BE SURE TO STRIKE THE BALL FIRST!

THE "BOUNCE AND ROLL" SHOT

SOME SITUATIONS RULE OUT A HIGH PITCH APPROACH: A TOO-CLOSE LIE, A MOUND GUARDING A TIGHT PIN POSITION, OVERHANGING LIMBS, ETC. THIS KIND OF PROBLEM CALLS FOR A LOW BOUNCE AND ROLL SHOT WITH A CHOKED-UP LONG IRON.

POSITION THE BALL NEAR YOUR RIGHT FOOT, ADDRESSING IT SO AS TO EMPHASIZE THE DOWNWARD CHARACTER OF THE BLOW. USE AN ABBREVIATED BUT FIRM SWING, AND FOLLOW THROUGH AS MUCH AS THE "HIT" DEMANDS.

SAFETY FIRST!

WINNING IN STROKE PLAY LIKELY DOES NOT DEPEND UPON ANY ONE SHOT AS IN MATCH PLAY, SO **SAFETY FIRST** SHOULD GET THE NOD OVER **TEMPTATION** WHEN YOU ARE FACED WITH A "RISKY" SHOT.

FOR INSTANCE... IF YOU'RE FACED WITH A DELICATE RECOVERY SHOT TO A CLOSE PIN GUARDED BY A DEEP, WIDE TRAP -- YOUR BEST SHOT IS TO PLAY WELL BEYOND THE TROUBLE AND ACCEPT THE PROBABLE BOGEY (OR HOPE FOR A ONE-PUTT).

IT'S EASY TO HAVE A <u>GOOD</u> ROUND COMPLETELY SPOILED BY **ONE** RISKY SHOT THAT "FAILED"!

CHOOSING A 9-IRON OVER A WEDGE

IF YOU FIND YOURSELF WEDGE DISTANCE AWAY FROM THE GREEN AND FACING A HEADWIND, A 9-IRON PROBABLY WOULD BE THE BEST CLUB TO PLAY.

LESS LOFT MEANS GREATER CONTROL, ESPECIALLY WHEN PLAYING IN THE WIND.

WHERE YOU WOULD NORMALLY USE A 3/4 SWING WITH THE WEDGE, PLAY ABOUT A 1/2 SWING 9-IRON AND KEEP THE BALL LOW. STOPPING IT WILL BE NO PROBLEM WITH THE HEADWIND.

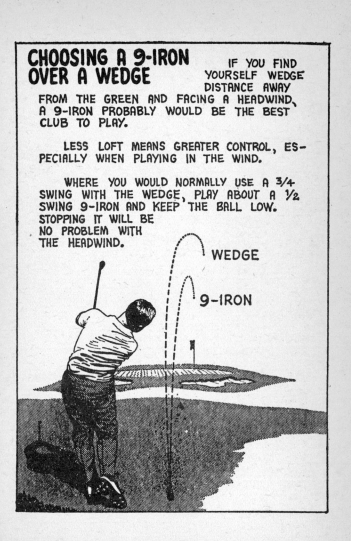

WEDGE

9-IRON

THE VERSATILE "SAND WEDGE"

THE SAND WEDGE SHOULD NOT BE LIMITED TO BUNKER DUTY ALONE. THERE ARE MANY INSTANCES AROUND THE GREEN WHERE IT SHOULD BE CONSIDERED FOR PLAYING OFF THE GRASS...ESPECIALLY WHEN YOU NEED TO STOP A PITCH QUICKLY ON THE GREEN.

THIS SHOT IS USED EXTENSIVELY BY THE TOURING PROFESSIONALS. IT GETS THE BALL UP QUICKLY AND HITS THE PUTTING SURFACE WITH LITTLE RUN, WHEREAS THE PITCHING WEDGE ONLY TAKES THE BITE ON THE SECOND OR THIRD HOP.

HITTING THE SHORT IRON FROM THE ROUGH

PLAY THIS SHOT AS YOU WOULD A REGULAR APPROACH FROM THE FAIRWAY, EXCEPT OPEN THE CLUBFACE SLIGHTLY AT ADDRESS -- SINCE THE ROUGH HAS A TENDENCY TO CLOSE THE CLUBFACE JUST BEFORE IMPACT.

HOLD YOUR LEFT HAND FIRM THROUGHOUT THE SWING....AND APPLY A LITTLE MORE EFFORT THAN FOR A NORMAL SHORT IRON SHOT.

ABOUT THE THREE-QUARTER SWING

IT IS COMMON KNOWLEDGE THAT MANY GOLFERS SHUN THE THREE-QUARTER SWING BECAUSE THEY BELIEVE THEMSELVES PRONE TO MISS THE SHOT WHENEVER THEY "LET UP." THIS IS TAKING THE WRONG VIEW OF AN IMPORTANT SHOT ADAPTABLE FOR WIND-PLAY AND OTHER OCCASIONS.

IT CALLS NOT SO MUCH FOR AN EASY SWING AS FOR A SHORT SWING -- THREE-QUARTER LENGTH RATHER THAN THREE-QUARTER POWER. SIMPLY CHOKE UP SOME FOR A BETTER "FEEL", AND HIT IT AS HARD AT IMPACT AS USUAL!

PRACTICING
WITH SHORT IRONS

I AGREE WITH THE ADVOCATION OF MOST GOLF INSTRUCTORS ON THE IMPORTANCE OF GENEROUS SHORT-IRON PRACTICE. BUT TO TRULY IMPROVE THESE "FINESSE" CLUBS, PRACTICE HALF AND THREE-QUARTER SHOTS AS WELL AS FULL ONES.

IN OTHER WORDS, PRACTICE HITTING YOUR 7-IRON THE SAME DISTANCE AS A FULL 9-IRON SHOT, ETC. THIS PHASE OF PRACTICE IS ESPECIALLY VALUABLE FOR OVER-ALL FEEL AND TOUCH OF THESE CLUBS, AND ADDS CONFIDENCE IN ANTICIPATING SHOTS INTO THE WIND AND UNDER OTHER UNCOMMON SITUATIONS.

CHAPTER 6

Out of the Sand

To most average golfers, playing a shot out of the sand remains something of a mystery. They watch with envy bordering on awe how seasoned pros consistently blast their way out, and they are left with the illusion that there is some secret to good bunker play.

There is no such secret. Everyone who plays golf is privy to the same knowledge. How well you play your way out of sand depends on how well you have absorbed the primers and how much application you've given them. The only mystery I find in playing from a trap is why more average golfers aren't better at it than they are.

I've always felt that good sand shots were so vital to your game that I make a special point of stressing it when I talk to young players. During the course of a single round you could find yourself in a trap maybe half a dozen times. Each trap could present a slightly different golf problem, so the outcome of your score could very probably hinge on how well you can extricate yourself.

Some of the testier bunker shots I cover in this section include hitting the long explosion, playing from wet, soggy sand, and coming out of a buried lie. But I didn't neglect some of the more common examples, which still give an alarming number of competent players great difficulty.

While there are some general rules that apply to all shots from the sand, such as taking a good, firm stance, swinging slower than usual, and opening the blade of your club, there are other little tips that I hope you'll find useful. Only putting them to frequent use will tell.

· DIGGING IN ·

IF YOU HAVE WATCHED PROFESSIONALS LIVE OR ON TELEVISION THEN I AM SURE YOU HAVE SEEN THEM SQUIRM AROUND AND DIG IN SO MUCH WHEN FACED WITH A SAND TRAP SHOT THAT IT APPEARED THEY WANTED TO HIT IT OUT WITH THEIR ELBOWS!

ACTUALLY, WHEN ON THE SUBJECT OF SAND PLAY I CANNOT OVEREMPHASIZE THE IMPORTANCE OF "DIGGING IN" SATISFACTORILY WITH YOUR FEET AS YOU TAKE YOUR STANCE. NOT ONLY DO YOU GET A FIRM FOOTING, BUT YOU CAN GET A GOOD IDEA OF THE TEXTURE OF THE SAND.

'SLOW DOWN' FOR TRAP SHOTS

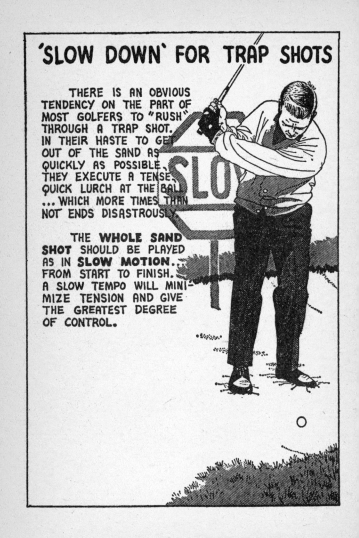

THERE IS AN OBVIOUS TENDENCY ON THE PART OF MOST GOLFERS TO "RUSH" THROUGH A TRAP SHOT. IN THEIR HASTE TO GET OUT OF THE SAND AS QUICKLY AS POSSIBLE, THEY EXECUTE A TENSE, QUICK LURCH AT THE BALL ... WHICH MORE TIMES THAN NOT ENDS DISASTROUSLY.

THE **WHOLE SAND SHOT** SHOULD BE PLAYED AS IN **SLOW MOTION**. FROM START TO FINISH. A SLOW TEMPO WILL MINI-MIZE TENSION AND GIVE THE GREATEST DEGREE OF CONTROL.

TAKE THE "SURE" WAY OUT

WHENEVER YOU FIND YOUR BALL CLOSE TO AN EXTREMELY STEEP BUNKER LIP...BLASTING FOR THE CUP USUALLY OFFERS BUT A SLIGHT CHANCE FOR SUCCESS. TAKE THE SURE WAY OUT -- AN ALTERNATE ROUTE -- EVEN IF IT MEANS DIRECTING YOUR SHOT 20 TO 30 FEET TO THE LEFT OR RIGHT OF THE HOLE!

LEAVING A LONGER PUTT CERTAINLY BEATS WASTING UNNECESSARY STROKES IN ATTEMPTING A "MIRACLE SHOT."

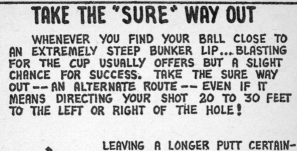

THE DOWNHILL TRAP SHOT

TRY TO SET YOUR BODY FOR THIS SHOT IN SUCH A MANNER AS TO BE AS PARALLEL AS POSSIBLE TO THE ANGLE OF THE SLOPE. BE CAREFUL THAT EACH FOOT -- THE LEFT ONE PARTICULARLY -- IS WELL PLANTED TO AVOID ANY SLIPPING ON THE DOWNSWING.

PLAY THE BALL NEARER THE RIGHT FOOT, SINCE THE BOTTOM OF YOUR SWING WILL BE REACHED SOONER THAN USUAL. TAKE THE CLUB BACK **ABRUPTLY** AND BRING IT DOWN SHARPLY BEHIND THE BALL ... FOLLOWING THE GENERAL CONTOUR OF THE SLOPE ON THE FOLLOW-THROUGH.

HITTING THE LONG TRAP SHOT

FAIRWAY BUNKERS ARE A NEMESIS TO ALL GOLFERS, BUT THEIR TREACHERY CAN BE REDUCED IF YOU WILL DEVELOP AN **ESCAPE** SHOT.

CHOOSE ENOUGH CLUB TO CLEAR THE FRONT LIP OF THE TRAP. <u>CHOKE UP</u> ON THE CLUB (SINCE THE BALL IS CLOSER TO YOU IN SAND), PLANT YOUR FEET SOLIDLY, AND AIM AT THE <u>TOP</u> OF THE BALL.

TRY TO USE A SLIGHTLY MORE **UPRIGHT** SWING FOR THIS SHOT.

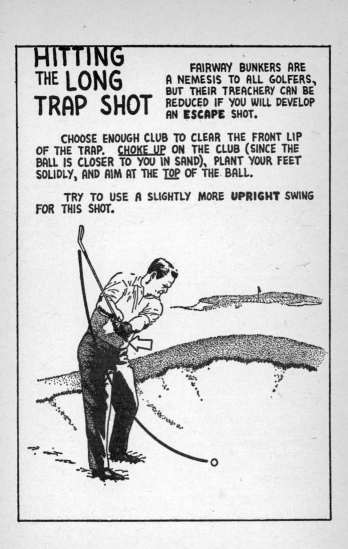

CHIPPING OUT OF SAND

IF TRAP CONDITIONS ARE SUITABLE A CHIP SHOT IS BETTER THAN EXPLODING WITH THE WEDGE. IF THERE IS LITTLE OR NO LIP, AND THE PIN IS WAY BACK ON THE GREEN.... THEN TAKE THE 8 OR 9 IRON INTO THE TRAP.

PLAY THE BALL OFF THE RIGHT HEEL, CHOKE UP ON YOUR GRIP, AND HOOD THE FACE SLIGHTLY.

THEN, WITH A STEADY HEAD, HIT **DOWN** FIRMLY ON THE BALL WITHOUT HITTING ANY SAND UNTIL AFTER IMPACT.

THE 'SOGGY' SAND SHOT

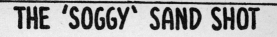

THIS SCARY-LOOKING SHOT IS ACTUALLY EASIER TO PLAY THAN FROM DRY SAND.

POSITION THE BALL OFF YOUR LEFT HEEL WITH YOUR SAND-WEDGE FACE **WIDE OPEN.** MAKE A SHORT, **OUTSIDE** AND **LOW** BACKSWING.... THEN HIT ABOUT AN INCH BEHIND THE BALL. THE CUSHIONING EFFECT OF DAMP SAND, PLUS YOUR LOW SWING ARC AND OPEN FACE WILL KEEP THE CLUBFACE FROM DIGGING IN TOO DEEPLY.

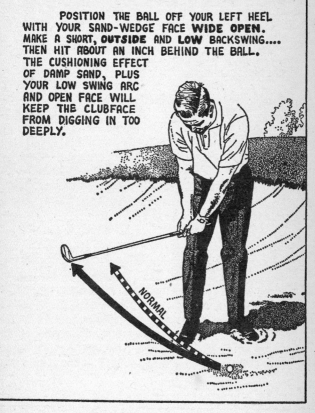

NORMAL

CHAPTER 7

On the Green

The phrase "getting down in two" is one of the most common in golf. It aptly refers to the golfer's goal of getting the ball in the cup in two strokes once he's on the green or just off it. For putting is the bread-and-butter part of the game, and no matter how often we may get down in two, the quest continues in our constant struggle against par.

The first thing I always stress in putting is being comfortable. This is not as simple as it sounds. Being comfortable does not mean being relaxed. By comfortable, I mean taking a stance from which you can putt well consistently. From my own experience, I can tell you that I change my stance whenever I find myself putting poorly. One time I may putt from a rather narrow stance; another time I may change to a wider stance. It all depends on how I am putting at the moment. If your current putting stance is working for you, stick with it. If not, try to adjust to a new one that makes you feel comfortable but not so loose that it will cause you to lose control of your putting stroke.

Another phase of putting about which I have to keep reminding myself is keeping the head of my putter traveling in a straight path. Again, this is something that may seem quite elemental, but you'd be surprised how easy it is to forget when your mind is contemplating other matters. We all have a tendency to concentrate so hard on the distance and line of a putt that we neglect to check the face of the putter. Quite often we miss seemingly easy putts because the putter isn't moving in a straight line. Keep it straight and you'll sink the easy ones, as well as the harder ones.

FOR THE BEGINNER:
THE PUTTING GRIP

THE DESIRED PUTTING GRIP SHOULD PLACE BOTH HANDS IN SUCH A WAY AS TO KEEP THE PUTTER FACE SQUARE TO THE LINE DURING THE ENTIRE STROKE.

I PREFER THE **REVERSE OVERLAP.** THIS GRIP PLACES ALL FOUR FINGERS OF THE RIGHT HAND ON THE CLUB AND KEEPS THE RIGHT HAND BEHIND THE SHAFT (WITH THE PALM SQUARE TO THE LINE), ENABLING IT TO "PUSH" THE PUTTER HEAD RIGHT AT THE HOLE.

THE BACK OF MY "GUIDING" LEFT HAND IS TURNED JUST SLIGHTLY TO THE LEFT (OF BEING SQUARE TO THE LINE) SO AS TO MAKE PULLING DIFFICULT.

FOR THE BEGINNER:
PUTTING
STANCE AND STROKE

JUST AS WITH THE PUTTING GRIP, PUTTING <u>STANCE</u> AND <u>STROKE</u> ARE HIGHLY **INDIVIDUAL.**

I GET BEST RESULTS FROM A REASONABLY **SQUARE** STANCE... PLAYING THE BALL ON A LINE WITH A POINT BETWEEN THE TOES AND ARCH OF MY LEFT FOOT. I TRY TO KEEP MY HEAD BEHIND THE BALL.. AND FEEL THAT I'M LOOKING DOWN THE LINE FROM BEHIND RATHER THAN FROM THE TOP OF THE BALL.

I TRY TO **STROKE,** NOT PUNCH, THE BALL. I SWING BACK AND THROUGH SMOOTHLY WITH **BOTH** HANDS.

THE "RIGHT ELBOW" IN PUTTING

I USE MY RIGHT ELBOW AS SORT OF A FULCRUM, OR GUIDE, TO STABILIZE MY PUTTING STROKE.

I FIND THAT BY HOLDING MY RIGHT ELBOW CLOSE TO MY **RIGHT SIDE** <u>THROUGHOUT</u> THE STROKE I CAN KEEP THE PUTTER FACE SQUARE AND MOVING STEADILY ON THE <u>LINE OF DIRECTION</u>.

WHEN THE RIGHT ELBOW STRAYS FROM THE SIDE, THE PUTTER FACE TENDS TO CLOSE AND TRAVELS OUTSIDE THE DIRECTIONAL LINE.. RESULTING IN A PULLED PUTT.

FOR THE BEGINNER:
PROPER WEIGHT DISTRIBUTION IN PUTTING

THE CORRECT DISTRI-
BUTION OF WEIGHT IN
PUTTING IS THE ONE
WHICH ALLOWS YOUR HEAD,
BODY AND SHOULDERS TO
REMAIN PERFECTLY STILL
THROUGHOUT THE STROKE.

I FEEL THAT MORE
WEIGHT ON THE LEFT
FOOT -- OR LEFT HEEL,
PREFERABLY -- OFFERS
THE EASIEST WAY OF
ACHIEVING A STABLE
POSITION.

HOW TO ACHIEVE
PROPER DISTRIBUTION
IS PERSONAL .... JUST
BE SURE TO CARRY
YOUR WEIGHT AS NAT-
URAL AND COMFORTABLE
AS POSSIBLE.

FOR THE BEGINNER:
YOUR PUTTING STYLE

CHOOSE YOUR OWN STYLE OF PUTTING, WHETHER IT BE THE **UPRIGHT** OR **CROUCHED** POSITION OF THE BODY.

COMFORT AND VANTAGE OF THE LINE SHOULD BOTH BE CONSIDERED. IN MY OWN CASE, THE MOST COMFORTABLE POSITION -- AND THE ONE FROM WHICH I CAN BEST FIND THE LINE -- IS A CROUCHED POSITION. I FEEL THAT WHEN I AM DOWN LOW I AM ABLE TO LOOK FROM **BEHIND** THE BALL AND SEE THE LINE MORE CLEARLY.

FOR THE BEGINNER:
CHOICE
OF
PUTTER

FIND A PUTTER THAT GIVES YOU THE BEST **FEEL**, THEN... STICK WITH IT. TOO OFTEN A GOLFER WILL CHANGE PUTTERS WHEN HIS TROUBLE ON THE GREEN IS NOT HIS PUTTER AT ALL (IT'S USUALLY **HIM**).

IF YOUR COURSE HAS FAST GREENS, A LIGHT PUTTER WOULD BE BEST. A HEAVIER PUTTER, ON THE OTHER HAND, IS USUALLY THE MOST APPROPRIATE ON SLOW GREENS.

PUTTING ON FAST GREENS

CAUTIOUS PUTTING AND THOUGHTFUL PUTTING ARE MORE IMPORTANT THAN EVER ON REAL FAST GREENS. IT IS HIGHLY ADVANTAGEOUS TO LEAVE YOURSELF WITH MORE UPHILL OR STRAIGHT-IN PUTTS..EVEN A FEW SIDEHILL PUTTS.. RATHER THAN THOSE DANGEROUS DOWNHILLERS!

DOWNHILL PUTTS ON FAST GREENS CAN SLIDE AWAY FROM THE HOLE SO EASILY AND PUT YOU IN A PRE-CARIOUS POSITION FOR A THREE-PUTT GREEN. SO·A LITTLE FORETHOUGHT PAYS BIG DIVIDENDS ON FAST GREENS.

USING THE "TEXAS WEDGE"

THIS CATCHY PHRASE REFERS TO USE OF THE PUTTER INSTEAD OF A CHIPPING OR PITCHING CLUB ON DELICATE LITTLE SHOTS AROUND THE GREEN. IF THE CONDITIONS ARE RIGHT (FIRM TURF THAT IS FREE FROM WET OR HEAVY GRASS) THE PERCENTAGES FAVOR THE USE OF THE PUTTER....ESPECIALLY FROM THIN LIES.

USE YOUR NORMAL PUTTING STROKE ON THIS SHOT AND HIT IT JUST A LITTLE HARDER THAN ON A REGULAR PUTT. REMEMBER TOO, AS ALWAYS, TO KEEP YOUR HEAD DOWN!

AVOIDING THE THREE-PUTT

IT IS ONLY NATURAL THAT MOST THREE-PUTTS TAKE PLACE ON THOSE LONG 30-AND 40-FOOTERS. HOWEVER, I BELIEVE THEY CAN BE REDUCED WITH EMPHATIC CONCENTRATION ON **DISTANCE**, AND NOT AS MUCH THOUGHT TOWARD GRAIN DIRECTION AND CONTOURS.

CERTAINLY YOU WANT TO CHOOSE A GENERAL LINE FOR YOUR PUTT...BUT THEN CONCENTRATE ON PROPER <u>SPEED</u> AND <u>DISTANCE</u>. THE RESULTING EFFORT SHOULD PUT YOU CLOSE ENOUGH FOR AN EASY SECOND PUTT.

DO YOUR OWN THINKING ON THE GREEN

FRIENDLY ADVICE IS USUALLY THE MOST ABUNDANT AND CHEAPEST ENTITY ON A GOLF COURSE. HOWEVER, A TIME TO "SHUT OUT THE WORLD" IS DURING THE PREPARATION FOR A PUTT.

ALWAYS LINE UP YOUR OWN PUTTS. NO ONE ELSE KNOWS HOW HARD YOU ARE GOING TO HIT THE BALL, AND THUS CANNOT INSTRUCT YOU AS TO THE BREAK. AND ANYWAY, A LOT OF "DISCUSSION" ON A BREAK HAS A TENDENCY TO DISTRACT ATTENTION FROM **DISTANCE**!

BEATING THE BERMUDA BREAK

A CAREFUL ANALYSIS OF THE GRAIN DIRECTION ON BERMUDA-GRASS GREENS CAN ELIMINATE MANY MISSED "LEVEL" PUTTS THAT ACTUALLY BREAK!

FINDING THE SILVERY SHEEN VIEW OF THE GRASS WILL LOCATE THE DOWNGRAIN DIRECTION. IF YOUR PUTT <u>CROSSES</u> THIS GRAIN, THEN ALLOW SOME BREAK AS IF YOU WERE PUTTING ON A GENTLE SLOPE.

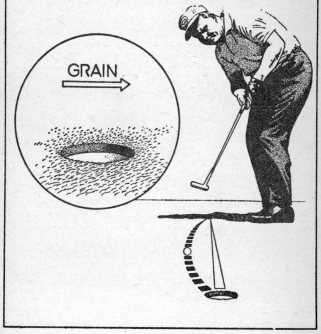

GRAIN

FOLLOW·THROUGH ON PUTTS TOO

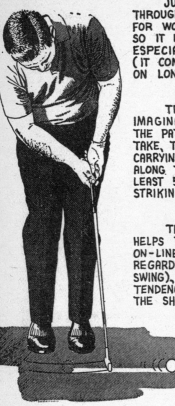

JUST AS THE FOLLOW-THROUGH IS NECESSARY FOR WOOD AND IRON SHOTS, SO IT IS FOR PUTTS.... ESPECIALLY ON SHORT ONES (IT COMES MORE NATURAL ON LONG PUTTS).

TRY TO DRAW AN IMAGINARY LINE ALONG THE PATH THE BALL WILL TAKE, THEN CONCENTRATE ON CARRYING THE PUTTER FACE ALONG THIS LINE FOR AT LEAST 5 INCHES AFTER STRIKING THE BALL.

THIS FOLLOW-THROUGH HELPS TO ASSURE A SOLID, ON-LINE PUTT (ALMOST REGARDLESS OF THE BACK-SWING), AND LESSENS THE TENDENCY TO "QUIT" ON THE SHORT ONES.